MARXISM

&

CHRISTIANITY

ALASDAIR MACINTYRE

SECOND EDITION

DUCKWORTH

This impression 2001
Second edition 1995
First published in 1968 by
Gerald Duckworth & Co. Ltd.
61 Frith Street, London W1D 3JL
Tel: 020 7434 4242
Fax: 020 7434 4420
Email: inquiries@duckworth-publishers.co.uk
www.ducknet.co.uk

A catalogue record for this book is available
from the British Library

ISBN 0 7156 2673 6

Printed in Great Britain by
Antony Rowe Ltd, Eastbourne

CONTENTS

1. 1953 from the standpoint of 1995

When the first version of this book was published in 1953, under the title *Marxism: an Interpretation* (London: SCM Press), Stalin was not yet dead and the Cold War had already taken determinate form. In February 1953 NATO created a unified military command. In June the Soviet suppression of a workers' rising in East Berlin exemplified the ruthless subordination of the whole of Eastern Europe to Soviet interests. It had already long been part of the stock-in-trade of many Western apologists to accept at its face-value the Soviet Union's claim that its social, political and economic practice embodied Marxist theory, in order to justify their own root-and-branch rejection of Marxism. And it was generally, if not universally, taken for granted among both theologians and ordinary church-goers that, because Marxism was an atheistic materialism, and because persecution by Soviet

[v]

power was designed to deny, so far as it could, any independence to the lives of the churches, Christianity had to identify itself with the cause of the anticommunist West. It was of course true that some parts of Marxist theory and some Marxist predictions had genuinely been discredited. It was also true that Christian orthodoxy could not but oppose that in Marxism which was either a ground for or a consequence of its atheism. But the simple-minded wholesale anticommunist rejection of Marxism and the equally simple-minded understanding of the relationship between Marxism and Christianity as one of unqualified antagonism exaggerated and distorted these truths in the interests of the then dominant Western ideology.

It was against what I took in 1953 and still take in 1995 to be these distortions that I asserted the central thesis of this book: that Marxism does not stand to Christianity in any relationship of straightforward antagonism, but rather, just because it is a transformation of Hegel's secularized version of Christian theology, has many of the characteristics of a Christian heresy rather than of non-Christian unbelief. Marxism is in consequence a doctrine with the same metaphysical and moral scope as Christianity and it is the only secular postenlightenment doctrine to have such a scope. It proposes a mode of understanding nature and human nature, an account of the direction and meaning of history and of the standards by which right action is to be judged, and an explanation of error and of evil, each of these integrated into an overall worldview, a worldview that can only be made fully intelligible by understanding it as a transformation of Christianity. More than that, Marxism was and is a transformation of Christianity which, like some other heresies, provided grounds for reasserting elements in Christianity which had been ignored and obscured by many Christians. What elements are these? They are most aptly and relevantly identified by asking what attitude Christians ought to take to capitalism and then noting how that attitude relates to the Marxist analysis of capitalism.

What, on a Christian understanding of human and social relationships, does God require of us in those relationships? That we love our neighbours and that we recognize that charity towards them goes beyond, but always includes justice. An adequate regard for justice always involves not only a concern that justice be done and injustice prevented or remedied on any particular occasion, but also resistance to and, where possible, the abolition of institutions that systematically generate injustice. Christians have far too often behaved badly – thereby confirming what Christianity teaches about sinfulness – in failing to recognize soon enough and to respond to the evils of such institutions. Long after the evils of North American and Latin American slavery and the possibility of abolishing it should have been plain to them, too many Christians remained blind to those evils. And when the wickedness of Fascism and that of National Socialism were all too apparent, too many Christians refused to acknowledge them, let alone to engage in resistance. We therefore do well to honour those who did understand what charity and justice required: such Christians as the Dominican, Bartolomé de Las Casas, the evangelical Anglicans, John Newton and William Wilberforce, the Lutheran, Dietrich Bonhoeffer, the Catholics, Edith Stein and Maximilian Kolbe and Franz Jägerstetter.

For the same reasons we ought also to honour those Christian laity and clergy, a very small minority, who recognized relatively early the systematic injustices generated by nascent and developed commercial and industrial capitalism. Those evils were and are of two kinds. There is on the one hand the large range of particular injustices perpetrated against individuals and groups on this or that particular occasion, where those other individuals who committed the injustices could have done otherwise consistently with conformity to the standards of profit and loss, of commercial and industrial success and failure, enforced by and in a capitalist economic and social order. The immediate cause of such injustices lies in the character of those individuals who commit them. But there is on the other hand a type of injustice which is not the work of a particular person on a particular occasion, but is instead perpetrated institutionally.

Such injustice has a number of distinct, if closely related aspects. There is the source of injustice that confronts every individual or group at the point at which they first encountered the capitalist system, usually by entering the labour market, from the period of nascent capitalism onwards. This source of injustice arises from the gross inequalities in the initial appropriation of capital – whatever point in time is taken to be the initial point – an appropriation that was in significant part the outcome of acts of force and fraud by the appropriators. This inequality in the relationship of those with capital to those without it is much more than the inequality between rich and poor that is to be found in the vast majority of societies. In many premodern social orders, just because the poor provide products and services that the rich need, there is still something of a reciprocal relationship between rich and poor, governed by customary standards. And in such societies characteristically the poor will have, and be recognized as entitled to, their own resources: a share of the product of the land they work, customary rights over common land, and the like. But the relationship of capital to labour is such that it inescapably involves an entirely one-sided dependence, except insofar as labour rebels against its conditions of work. The more effective the employment of capital, the more labour becomes no more than an instrument of capital's purposes, and an instrument whose treatment is a function of the needs of long-term profit maximization and capital formation.

The relationships which result are the impersonal relationships imposed by capitalist markets upon all those who participate in them. What is necessarily absent in such markets is any justice of desert. Concepts of a just wage and a just price necessarily have no application to transactions within those markets. Hard, skilled and conscientious work, if it does not generate sufficient profit, something that it is not in the power of the worker to determine, will always be apt to be rewarded by unemployment. It becomes impossible for workers to understand their work as a contribution to the common good of a society which at the economic level no longer has a common good, because of the different and conflicting interests of different classes. The needs of capital formation impose upon capitalists and upon those who manage their enterprises a need to extract from the work of their employees a surplus which is at the future disposal of capital and not of labour. It is of course true that the fact that the profitability of an enterprise in the longer run requires a relatively stable and, so far as possible, satisfied labour force means that such exploitation must sometimes, to be effective over time, be tempered and assume a relatively benign face. And it is clearly much, much better that capitalism should provide a rising standard of living for large numbers of people than that it should not. But no amount of a rise in the standard of living by itself alters the injustice of exploitation. And the same is true of two other aspects of injustice.

Relationships of justice between individuals and groups require that the terms of their relationship be such that it is reasonable for those individuals and groups to consent to those terms. Contractual relationships imposed by duress are not genuinely contractual. So freedom to accept or reject particular terms of employment and freedom to accept or reject particular terms of exchange in free markets are crucial elements in those markets being in fact free. When in premodern societies markets are auxiliary to production that is not primarily for the market, but for local need, so that markets provide a useful means of exchange for what is surplus to local need, a means whereby all those who participate in them benefit, then the conditions of such freedom may be satisfied. And in a society of small productive units, in which everyone has an opportunity to own (and not indirectly through shareholdings) the means of production – the type of economy envisaged by Chesterton and other distributists – free markets will be a necessary counterpart to freedom of ownership and freedom of labour. (This is a type of economy which does in fact give expression to the understanding of human freedom of the encyclical *Centesimus Annus*, an encyclical whose exaggerated optimism about the actualities of contemporary capitalism, both in Eastern Europe and in the United States, has led to unfortunate misconstruals of its doctrine.) But in the markets of modern capitalism prices are often imposed by factors external to a particular market: those, for example, whose livelihood has been made subject to international market forces by their becoming exclusively producers for some product for which there was, but is no longer, international demand, will find themselves compelled to accept imposed low prices or even the bankruptcy of their economy. Market relationships in contemporary capitalism are for the most part relations imposed both on labour and on small producers, rather than in any sense freely chosen.

I have tried so far in this account of the injustice characteristic of capitalism to make it clear that, when apologists for capitalism point out quite correctly that capitalism has been able to generate material prosperity at a higher level and for more people than any other economic system in human history, what they say is irrelevant as a rebuttal of these charges of injustice. But the rising standard of material prosperity in capitalist economies is itself closely related to another aspect of their failure in respect of justice. It is not only that individuals and groups do not receive what they deserve, it is also that they are educated or rather miseducated to believe that what they should aim at and hope for is not what they deserve, but whatever they may happen to want. They are in the vast majority of cases to regard themselves primarily as consumers whose practical and productive activities are no more than a means to consumption. What constitutes success in life becomes a matter of the successful acquisition of consumer goods, and thereby that acquisitiveness which is so often a character trait necessary for success in capital accumulation is further sanctioned. Unsurprisingly *pleonexia*, the drive to have more and more, becomes treated as a central virtue. But Christian theologians in the middle ages had learned from Aristotle that *pleonexia* is the vice that is the counterpart to the virtue of justice. And they had understood, as later theologians have failed to do, the close connection between developing capitalism and the sin of usury. So it is not after all just general human sinfulness that generates particular individual acts of injustice over and above the institutional injustice of capitalism itself. Capitalism also provides systematic incentives to develop a type of character that has a propensity to injustice.

Finally we do well to note that, although Christian indictments of capitalism have justly focussed attention upon the wrongs done to the poor and the exploited, Christianity has to view any social and economic order that treats being or becoming rich as highly desirable as doing wrong to those who must not only accept its goals, but succeed in achieving them. Riches are, from a biblical point of view, an affliction, an almost insuperable obstacle to entering the kingdom of heaven. Capitalism is bad for those who succeed by its standards as well as for those who fail by them, something that many preachers and theologians have failed to recognize. And those Christians who have recognized it have often enough been at odds with ecclesiastical as well as political and economic authorities.

Notice now that this Christian critique of capitalism relied and relies in key part, even if only in part, upon concepts and theses drawn from Marxist theory. Just as Marxism learned certain truths from Christianity, so Christianity in turn needed and needs to learn certain truths from Marxism. But what does this mean for practice in general and for political practice in particular?

When I posed this question in 1953, I was able to find no satisfactory answer. Partly this was because I then aspired to an impossible condition: that of being genuinely and systematically a Christian, who was also genuinely and systematically a Marxist. I therefore tried to integrate elements of Christianity with elements of Marxism in the wrong way. But in so doing I was also in error in another respect. Among my as yet unquestioned assumptions was a belief that the only possible politics that could effectively respond to the injustices of a capitalist economic and social order was a politics that took for granted the institutional forms of the modern state and that had as its goal the conquest of state power, whether by electoral or by other means, so that I could not as yet recognize that those who make the conquest of state power their aim are always in the end conquered by it and, in becoming the instruments of the state, themselves become in time the instruments of one of the several versions of modern capitalism.

2. 1968 from the standpoint of 1995

Large as these errors were, they were not the matters on which I was in 1953 most fundamentally at a loss. In the first version of this book there was a chapter on philosophy and practice that was omitted when I revised it in

1968. That chapter was originally included because it attempted to pose what I had rightly recognized as the fundamental problem. It was later omitted because I had by then learnt that I did not know how to pose that problem adequately, let alone how to resolve it. So in 1968 I mistakenly attempted to bypass it. But it cannot be avoided. What is that problem?

Any adequate account of the relationship between Marxism and Christianity would have to embody and be justified in terms of some systematic standpoint on the major issues of moral and political philosophy and of related philosophical disciplines. By 1953 I had acquired not only from my Marxist teachers, both in and outside the Communist Party, but also from the writings of R.G. Collingwood, a conception of philosophy as a form of social practice embedded in and reflective upon other forms of social practice. What I did not then fully understand was that philosophy needs to be conceived as having at least a fourfold subject-matter and a fourfold task. There is first of all that which has to be learned empirically: the rules and standards, concepts, judgments, and modes of argumentative justification, actually embodied in or presupposed by the modes of activity which constitute the life of the social order in which one is participating. Secondly, there are the ways of understanding or misunderstanding those activities and the relevant rules and standards, concepts, judgments, and modes of argumentative justification that are dominant in that particular social order. Thirdly, there is the relationship between these two in respect of how far the second is an adequate, and how far an inadequate and distorting representation of the first. And finally there is that of which a philosopher must give an account, if she or he is to vindicate the claim to have been able to transcend whatever limitations may have been imposed by her or his historical and social circumstances, at least to a sufficient extent to represent truly the first three and so to show not just how things appear to be from this or that historical and social point of view, but how things are.

Philosophy thus understood includes, but also extends a good deal beyond, what is taken to be philosophy on a conventional academic view of the disciplines. It is crucial to the whole philosophical enterprise, on any view of it, that its enquiries should be designed to yield a rationally justifiable set of theses concerning such familiar and central philosophical topics as perception and identity, essence and existence, the nature of goods, what is involved in rule-following and the like. But, from the standpoint towards which Marx and Collingwood had directed me, the discovery of such theses was valuable not only for its own sake, but was also needed to serve the further purpose of enabling us to understand about particular forms of social life what it is that, in some cases, enables those who participate in them to understand their own activities, so that the goods which they pursue are genuine goods, and, in others, generates systematic types of misunderstanding, so that those who participate in them by and large misconceive their good and are frustrated in its achievement.

Marx, for example, in his analysis of *bürgerlich* society, had shown how the characteristic forms of thought of that society at once articulate and disguise its underlying structure, and some of his heirs both within and outside Marxism – I think especially of both Karl Mannheim and Karl Polanyi – have since developed his insights further. But Marx and Engels were both blind to the extent to which their own thought not only has the marks characteristic of *bürgerlich* theorizing, but was distorted in a characteristically *bürgerlich* manner, notably in their treatment of *the* economic, *the* political, and *the* ideological as distinct and separate, albeit causally interrelated areas of human activity, a treatment whose effect was to transform contingent characteristics of mid- and late-nineteenth-century capitalist societies into analytical categories purporting to provide the key to human history and social structure in general.

By 1968 my reading of Lukacs had taught me to

recognize this fact and with it the general form of a central problem for any philosophical enquiry conceived as I was beginning to conceive it: how is it possible to identify in the case of other and rival theses and arguments a variety of distortions and limitations deriving from their authors' historical and social context, while at the same time being able to exhibit one's own theses and arguments, including one's theses and arguments about their theses and arguments, as exempt from such distortion and limitation? This was a question that had of course already been asked and answered by Hegel, by Marx and by numerous others. But by 1968 1 knew that not only their answers, but also their detailed formulations of the questions were vulnerable to insuperable objections.

Because I did not as yet know how to formulate this question adequately enough even to know where to look for an answer to it, I found myself distanced from identification with any substantive point of view. Whereas in 1953 I had, doubtless naively, supposed it possible to be in some significant way both a Christian and a Marxist, I was by 1968 able to be neither, while acknowledging in both standpoints a set of truths with which I did not know how to come to terms. In the case of Marxism, my reaction to recurrent attempts to reinstate Marxism as both economic and political theory and as *weltanschauung* had led me for a considerable time to reject more than I should have done; for redirecting my thought I am much indebted to conversations with George Lichtheim, Heinz Lubasz, Linda Nicholson, Marx Wartofsky and Cheney Ryan, who provided a variety of illuminating perspectives on the problems of Marxism. One result is that I would not now endorse what I wrote dismissively about the labour theory of value in 1953 and I would want to say considerably more on a number of topics, including the theory of value, than I did in 1968.

Christianity had become problematic for me as a consequence of my having supposed that the theology in terms of which its claims had to be understood was that of Karl Barth. But what Barth's theology proved unable to provide was any practically adequate account of the moral life, and, although I should have known better, I mistakenly took what is a defect in Barth's theology to be a defect of Christianity as such. This judgment seemed to be confirmed by the platitudinous emptiness of liberal Christian moralizing, whether Protestant or Catholic, a type of moralizing in which the positions of secular liberalism reappeared in various religious guises. And this liberalism, the moral and political counterpart and expression of developing capitalism, I rejected just as I had done in 1953 and for the same reasons.

Why is political liberalism to be rejected? The self-image of the liberal is after all that of a protagonist of human rights and liberties. Those liberals who are social democrats aspire to construct institutions in the trade union movement and the welfare state that will enable workers to participate in capitalist prosperity. And it would be absurd to deny that the achievement of pensions, health services and unemployment benefits for workers under capitalism has always been a great and incontrovertible good. Why then did and do I reject liberal social democracy? For at least three reasons. First, Marxist theorists had predicted that, if trade unions made it their only goal to work for betterment within the confines imposed by capitalism and parliamentary democracy, the outcome would be a movement towards first the domestication and then the destruction of effective trade union power. Workers would so far as possible be returned to the condition of mere instruments of capital formation. In both 1953 and 1968 I took this prediction to be warranted, although it was then treated with great contempt by the theorists of liberal social democracy. Since then it has of course turned out to be true.

Secondly, liberalism is the politics of a set of elites, whose members through their control of party machines and of the media, predetermine for the most part the range of political choices open to the vast mass of ordinary voters. Of those voters, apart from the making of electoral choices, passivity is required. Politics and their cultural ambiance have become areas of professionalized life, and among the most important of the relevant professionals are the professional manipulators of mass opinion. Moreover entry into and success in the arenas of liberal politics has increasingly required financial resources that only corporate capitalism can supply, resources that secure in return privileged access to those able to influence political decisions. Liberalism thus ensures for the most part the exclusion of most people from any possibility of active and rational participation in determining the form of community in which they live.

Thirdly, the moral individualism of liberalism is itself a solvent of participatory community. For liberalism in its practice as well as in much of its theory promotes a vision of the social world as an arena in which each individual, in pursuit of the achievement of whatever she or he takes to be her or his good, needs to be protected from other such individuals by the enforcement of individual rights. Moral argument within liberalism cannot therefore begin from some conception of a genuinely common good that is more and other than the sum of the preferences of individuals. But argument to, from and about such a conception of the common good is integral to the practice of participatory community. Hence if one holds that both justice as understood by St Paul and that justice which aspires to move from the maxim 'From each according to her or his ability, to each according to her or his contribution' to 'From each according to her or his ability, to each according to her or his need' can be embodied only in the internal and external relationships of participatory community, then liberalism will be incompatible with justice thus understood and will have to invent its own conceptions of justice, as it has indeed done.

When my grounds for rejecting liberalism are expressed in this way, it is evident that they presuppose a commitment to some set of positive affirmations. But these I did not in 1968 know how to formulate, in part because I did not know how to come to terms with either Marxism or Christianity and in part because I still lacked an adequate philosophical idiom for the statement, let alone the resolution of the relevant issues. So it was natural that for a considerable period I found it relatively easy to say what I was against, rather than what, if anything, I was for. Perceptive critics recognized some of my underlying commitments – hostile critics saw them as underlying credulities – better than I myself did.

Marxism and Christianity were themselves in continuing and striking transformation. The debates and the documents of the Second Vatican Council, which had met from 1962 to 1965, had by their definitive restatement of Christian doctrine provided resources for identifying both the negative legalism of theological conservatives and the vacuous moralism of theological liberals as twin distortions of faith and practice. But since the discussion and evaluation of the Council was all too often framed in terms of a set of conservative-liberal antitheses and so distorted by the very errors from which the Council should have delivered us and will perhaps in time deliver us, the immediate effect was one of apparent theological confusion. For Marxists many events of the late 1960s – the beginning of the Brezhnev era in the Soviet Union, the crushing by Soviet troops of the Czech project for socialism with a human face, the student uprisings, and the variously ineffective responses to those events of communist parties in France and Italy and of small sectarian Marxist groups – should have given further evidence of the systematic failure of Marxism as politics. Where Marxists were to be politically effective – as in the Communist Party of South Africa – it was always because they had adopted programmes and forms of action only connected with Marxism in the loosest and most indirect ways.

*

3. 1995

As I write, capitalism, taking a variety of forms that range from the corporate capitalism of the United States to the state capitalism of China, seems to be almost unchallenged worldwide – except of course by its own self-destructive and disillusioning tendencies. In the United States during a decade in which productivity has continually risen, the real wages of many types of worker have declined. The gap between richer and poorer has widened. When unemployment falls, this is treated as bad news on the stock market. Larger sections of the work force have become aware of their job insecurity, since profitability and capital formation require an ability to fire and to hire at will. In service industries many employees face continuing low-wage drudgery. Growth in technological expertise and in productive power have as their outcome societies of recurrently disappointed expectations, in which electorates, not knowing where to turn, exchange one set of political charlatans for another. In the world at large the crucial gap is that between the wealthy capitalist nations and their immediate satellites on the one hand and those now condemned to the poverty of exclusion and marginality in respect of international markets on the other.

In this situation what is most urgently needed is a politics of self-defence for all those local societies that aspire to achieve some relatively self-sufficient and independent form of participatory practice-based community and that therefore need to protect themselves from the corrosive effects of capitalism and the depredations of state power. And in the end the relevance of theorizing to practice is to be tested by what theorizing can contribute, indirectly or directly, to such a politics. At the very least we can hope for this from sound theoretical enquiry: that we become able to approach the political tasks of the present freed in some significant measure from some of the major errors that so often undermined anticapitalist politics in the past, in the hope that reopening enquiry and debate on issues and questions whose final resolution is widely supposed to have been achieved long since may turn out to be of a good deal more than academic interest. And so I have found it.

As early as the 1970s I had begun to formulate positions that would enable me to understand somewhat better not only what it was that had to be rejected in the moral, social and economic theory and practice of liberalism and individualism, but also how to evaluate in a more searching way the claims of Christian orthodoxy and the critique of Marxism. I came to recognize that the competing moral idioms in which contemporary ideologi-

cal claims, whether liberal or conservative, are framed –
the praise of Victorian values, various theories of natural
rights, Kantian universalism, contractarianism, utilitarianism – were the result of a fragmentation of practical
and evaluative discourse. Those competing moral idioms
were to be understood as the outcome of a history in
which different aspects of the life of practice had first
been abstracted from the practical and theoretical contexts in which they were at home and then transformed
into a set of rival theories, available for ideological deploy-
ment. What needed to be recovered, in order both to
understand this and to correct it, was some reconstructed
version of Aristotle's view of social and moral theory and
practice. I also understood better what type of community it was by contrast with which I had rightly found the
social relationships of both capitalist individualism and
Soviet command economies, very different as they were,
deformed and inadequate. The modes of social practice
in some relatively small-scale and local communities –
examples range from some kinds of ancient city and some
kinds of medieval commune to some kinds of modern
cooperative farming and fishing enterprises – in which
social relationships are informed by a shared allegiance
to the goods internal to communal practices, so that the
uses of power and wealth are subordinated to the
achievement of those goods, make possible a form of life

in which participants pursue their own goods rationally and critically, rather than having continually to struggle, with greater or lesser success, against being reduced to the status of instruments of this or that type of capital formation.

These were not two discoveries, but one, since what Aristotelian theory articulates are in fact the concepts embodied in and presupposed by such modes of practice, and such concepts themselves need to be understood in terms of their functioning within just those same modes of practice. Aristotle's statement of his own positions is of course at some points in need of greater or less revision and at others – in, for example, his treatment of women, productive workers and slavery – requires outright rejection. But the fruitful correction of these inadequacies and mistakes turned out to be best achieved by a better understanding of Aristotelian theory and practice. My realization that this was so was only one of several large consequences of my finally adopting what was a basically Aristotelian standpoint and then developing it in relation to contemporary issues inside and outside philosophy.

Having done so, I discovered that I had thereby discarded philosophical assumptions that had been at the root of my difficulties with substantive Christian orthodoxy. And the removal of these barriers was one, even if only one, necessary stage in my coming to acknowledge the truth of the biblical Christianity of the Catholic church. But I also understood better than I had done earlier not only what had been right in official Catholic condemnations of Marxism, but also how much had been mistaken and rooted in obfuscating and reactionary social attitudes. Part of what Catholic theologians – and more generally Christian theologians – had failed to focus upon sufficiently was the insistence by both Marx and Marxists on the close relationships of theory to practice, on how all theory, including all theology, is the theory of some mode or modes of practice. Just as the propositions of scientific theorizing are not to be either understood or evaluated in abstraction from their relationships to the practices of scientific enquiry within which they are proposed, revised and accepted or rejected, so it is too with other bodies of propositions. Detach any type of theorizing from the practical contexts in which it is legitimately at home, whether scientific, theological or political, and let it become a free-floating body of thought and it will be all too apt to be transformed into an ideology. So when Catholic theology is in good order, its peculiar work is to assist in making intelligible in a variety of contexts of practice what the church teaches authoritatively as the Word of God revealed to it and to the world. When and insofar as theology does not subordinate itself to that teaching, but claims independence of it, it becomes no more than one more set of competing religious opinions, sometimes perhaps opinions of great interest, but functioning very differently from theology in the service of the teaching church.

Marxism was proposed by its founders as a body of theory designed to inform, direct and provide self-understanding in the practice of working-class and intellectual struggle against capitalism. It too has recurrently become detached from such contexts of practice. When and insofar as it does so, it too becomes no more than a set of competing political, economic and social opinions. And of course its tendency towards degeneration into this condition is one of the marks of its failure. The errors and distortions that have afflicted Marxism are of course various and have a range of different causes, some of them deriving from the vicissitudes of its later history. But if we are now to learn how to criticize Marxism, not in order to separate ourselves from its errors and distortions – that phase should be long over – but in order once again to become able to learn from it, then we shall need once more to re-examine Marx's thought in the 1840s and above all the changes in his conception of the relationship of theory to practice. If we do so, we will have to recognize that Marxism was not so much defeated by criticisms from external standpoints, important as these certainly were, so much as it was self-defeated, defeated that is by the failures of both Marx and his successors to provide a resolution of key difficulties internal to Marxism.

Central among these was Marx's refusal or inability to press further some of the questions posed in and by the *Theses on Feuerbach* (for a first attempt to reopen such questions, even if only in a preliminary way, see my 'The *Theses on Feuerbach: A Road Not Taken*' in *Artifacts, Representations and Social Practice: Essays for Marx Wartofsky*, ed. R.S. Cohen and C.C. Gould, Dordrecht: Kluwer, 1994). And we need answers to these questions, if we are to be able to construct and sustain practice-based forms of local participatory community that will be able to survive the insidious and destructive pressures of contemporary capitalism and of the modern state. The politics of such communities and of the struggles to construct and sustain them will be much more effective if it is conducted by those able to understand and to learn from both Christianity and Marxism and to understand their relationship. If, even in a small way, this book contributes to such understanding and learning, then putting it into circulation for a third time will have been worthwhile.

January 1995   Alasdair MacIntyre

I.

SECULARIZATION AND THE ROLE OF MARXISM

> Christianity is the grandmother
> of Bolshevism.
>
> —O. SPENGLER

THE GREAT rationalist prophets of secularization, both during the eighteenth-century Enlightenment and after, have been proved wrong in at least two respects. First, the secularization of social life has been slower, less complete and less radical than they predicted. Not only has the last king not yet been strangled with the entrails of the last priest; it now looks as if the last king will be transmuted far less excitingly, if at all. And secondly, whereas the thinkers of the Enlightenment looked forward to a time when the superstitious interpretation of human existence embodied in Christianity would be replaced by a rational interpretation of man and nature, what has actually happened is that Christianity—insofar as it has lost its hold—has in advanced industrial communities not been replaced by anything at all. It is not, as the Enlightenment hoped, that the great questions about God and immortality, freedom and morality, to which religion once returned answers, now receive instead a new set of secular, atheistic answers. It is rather that the questions themselves are increasingly no longer asked, that men are largely deprived of any over-all interpretation of existence. They are not atheists or humanists in any active sense; they are merely not theists.

In this situation the small groups of self-styled humanists, gathered together in ethical societies and freethinking groups, the would-be successors of Voltaire and T. H. Huxley, present a picture of a pathetic kind, being on the whole less successful than the orthodox churches in gaining a hearing. Only one secular doctrine retains the scope of traditional religion in offering an interpretation of human existence by means of which men may situate themselves in the world and direct their actions to ends that transcend those offered by their immediate situation: Marxism. If for no other reason, Marxism would be of crucial importance. Why this is so can be thought out by considering what I intend by the expression "an interpretation of human existence."

Every individual finds himself with a given social

identity, a role or set of roles which define his phase within a set of social relationships, and these in turn constitute the immediate horizon of his life. Kinship, occupation, social class, each provide a set of descriptions from which individuals derive their identity as members of a society. It was Durkheim who saw that primitive religions present a concept of divinity in which the divine is a "collective representation" of the structure of social life; so that what the members of a society worship is the ensemble of their own social relationships in a disguised form. One need not suppose that this is the whole truth about religion to see that in a society of which Durkheim's thesis is true, the religious consciousness will be profoundly conservative. It will at once express and reinforce the social, political, and moral *status quo*. It is only insofar as religion ceases to be what Durkheim said it was that it can become an instrument of change. The great historical religions, as some Marxist writers have seen, have been rich enough *both* to express and to sanction the existing social structure *and* to provide a vision of an alternative, even if it was an alternative that could not be realized within the present world. Thus rival theologies within the same religion can sometimes express rival political visions of the world. So it clearly is with some Reformation and seventeenth-century

[3]

controversies. So it is with all those millenarian visions of a messianic reconstitution of society that have inspired primitive rebellion in so many forms.

But religion is only able to have this latter transforming function because and insofar as it enables individuals to identify and to understand themselves independently of their position in the existing social structure. It is in the contrast between what society tells a man he is and what religion tells him he is that he is able to find grounds both for criticizing the *status quo* and for believing that it is possible for him to act with others in changing it. For the most part lacking a religious perspective, the members of modern industrial societies have also mostly lacked any alternative framework of beliefs which would enable them to criticize and transform society. It is important to note, of course, that when radical political and social changes have taken place in religious forms and with religious inspiration, the gap between the kingdom of divine righteousness which believers hoped to establish and that social order which they actually succeed in establishing has been notable. Marx noted that "Cromwell and the English people had borrowed speech, passions and illusions from the Old Testament for their bourgeois revolutions. When the real aim had been achieved, when the bourgeois transformation of

English society had been accomplished, Locke succeeded Habakkuk."

So we can understand in general the attractions of the project of elaborating a secular doctrine of man and society that would have the scope and functions of religion, but would at the same time be rational in the sense that it would be open to amendment by critical reflection at every point, and that would enable men to self-consciously and purposefully achieve such transformations of social life as they wished to see. Such a doctrine becomes an urgent necessity when traditional religion ceases to provide an effective vision of the world for groups at once numerous and influential, and when their position in social life is such as to deprive them—really or apparently—of any stake in the social order. And it was precisely under these conditions, and to express and meet these needs, that Marxism arose.

It would be possible to advance the thesis that Marxism is an inheritor of some of the functions of Christianity in both a weaker and a stronger sense than I shall wish to do in this essay. The stronger thesis, an extremely familiar one, is that Marxism just *is* a religion or at least a theology, even if an atheistic one. The difficulty in holding this thesis is that its protagonists must be extremely selective in their attention to the phenomena: they can allow for the cult of Lenin, but scarcely for Lenin; and Stalinism becomes for them the paradigm of Marxism, which is as misleading as it would be to try to understand the nature of the New Testament by considering the attitudes and beliefs of the Emperor Constantine. But of course religious or quasi-religious attitudes and moods of belief do appear in the course of the history of Marxism, and if the thesis which I wish to present is correct, it will have some relevance to the explanation of these phenomena.

The weaker thesis is simply that Marxism inherited some of the functions of religion, without inheriting any of the content. This has certainly been the view of many Marxists. But it is impossible to understand the development of Marxist thought unless one understands it as continuous with and successive to the development of the philosophies of Hegel and Feuerbach; and one cannot understand these adequately unless one understands them as at least partially secular versions, or attempted secular versions, of the Christian religion. Thus Marxism shares in good measure both the content and the functions of Christianity as an interpretation of human existence, and it does so because it is the historical successor of Christianity. Or so I shall argue.

[6]

II.

FROM RELIGION TO PHILOSOPHY: HEGEL

> The criticism of religion is the beginning
> of all criticism.
> —KARL MARX

THE SIGNIFICANCE OF Hegel's thought is that it both
sums up the criticism of the Enlightenment while at
the same time transcending the Enlightenment's limitations, and introduces for the first time the themes
which dominate Marxist thinking. Hegel never quite
escaped the consequences of a theological education.
Yet Georg Lukacs, the Hungarian Marxist, is right in
stigmatizing the description of Hegel's early writings as theological as a "reactionary legend." Whence
this paradox? It springs from the fact that Hegel's
concern from the outset is with history, not with
theology, but that he approaches history with categories drawn from a religious background. The three
fundamental concepts in Hegel are "self-estrangement" or "alienation" (Selbst-Entfremdung), "objec-

tification" (Vergegenständlichung), and "coming to one's own" (Aneignung). "Self-estrangement" is a description of man in his fallen state. Men are divided against themselves and their fellows. This division is seen both in the conflicts within a man's thought and in the conflicts between man and man. Man does not obey the moral law that he makes for himself. He has a bad conscience as a result of this failure. He sees the moral law—the product of his own mind and will—set over against him, external to him. Man is at odds with the society of which he is a member, which indeed would not exist but for his participation. Because man does not live up to the standards of the society that he has made, he has a bad conscience with regard to it also. So he sees a conflict between himself and the society which he, and others like him, have created by their common participation. Society, created by individual men, is seen as set over against the individual man, in opposition to him. Society is external to him, just as law is. It is this externalization of what man has produced, this regarding as external objects what are in fact part of man's own being, that Hegel calls "objectification." To understand the world men must envisage what they perceive and try to comprehend as a set of objects. But in doing this they falsely reify their experience of the human world and treat people

[8]

and social institutions as if they were "things." This reification of the human world is a symptom of the estrangement of subject and object. Man has to overcome his self-estrangement. He is already on the way to doing this when he *recognizes* that he is alienated, a stranger in a world that he himself has made. The path back to self-knowledge and to being at one with one's self is what Hegel calls "appropriation" or "coming to one's own." What Hegel has done in forming these concepts is to take over certain aspects of Christian doctrine. St. Paul speaks of men being alienated in their thinking, and Hegel concentrates on this feature of man's condition as a fallen being rather than on other aspects of the fall. To be at one with one's self and other men is, in biblical terms, part of that atonement which Jesus brought. Hegel found a new use for a vocabulary originally framed to speak of sin and redemption; but why does he concentrate attention on these points and not on others? The answer is to be found in the historical problems which he used these concepts to elucidate.

In his early writings, Hegel is concerned with the contrast between ancient Greek religion and Christianity. The Greek city, as Hegel viewed it, had been both a religious and a political society. In it there was no such thing as the religion of the private individual, to be contrasted with the religion of society. This unity of the individual and the community was set in a context in which the divine and the human, the religious and the political were also one. There was no opposition between God and man to the Greek. Greek religion speaks of a divine immanence, and the state wherein the divine is immanent is a union of the individual and society. Sharply contrasted with this is the Christian world with its opposites of individual and society, of Church and State, where religion has become a concern of the private individual. God and man are now seen to be opposed conceptions and religion speaks of a divine transcendence. The question that Hegel puts in his early writings, the *Jugendschriften,* concerns the nature and significance of the transition from the Greek to the Christian world. The answer Hegel gives in these early writings is one that rests on his view of the relation of Jesus to Judaism. The Jewish nation are the people who have, more than any other, externalized the law: what is essentially written in the hearts of men is transmuted by them into the external observances of a written law. This objectification of the law is a consequence of their estrangement from man and nature, symbolized in the history of Abraham who left his kindred and was a wanderer, lacking all definite connection with persons or with places. The estrangement of the Jewish people has led them to objectify the law of their being. Against this Jesus preaches an inward law, written in the hearts of men, and so an overcoming of Jewish estrangement. But this preaching is rejected by the Jews. So Jesus puts aside the task of redeeming the nation and turns to the salvation of individuals by His preaching. This is the root, in Hegel's view, of the individualistic character of Christianity and in consequence of this individualism Christianity is a religion which has abjured the political and which opposes religious to political institutions. Thus within the Christian world there is an inheritance of estrangement and alienation which manifests itself in the conflicts of Church and society. Christianity has objectified the divine, set it over against this world and introduced a religion of otherworldliness and transcendence. Christianity contains symbols of man's ultimate reconciliation, of his coming to his own, but it is itself part of his estrangement. It cannot, for Hegel, be more than a clue to the nature of man's ultimate redemption.

The history of man's alienation and reconciliation is written by Hegel in the *Phenomenology of Mind*. The concepts of the *Phenomenology* are already more abstract than those of the *Jugend-*

schriften. "Mind" occupies a place which in the earlier writings was taken by the minds of concrete individuals. Indeed the *Phenomenology* is a history of "mind" or "spirit" (Geist), designed to bring out the way in which man's estrangement results in the loss of his freedom. For man is dominated by forces of nature and society which he does not recognize as the creations of his own spirit. Indeed his spirit in his estrangement is precisely not his own. Man in origin and in essence is a free being. In his estrangement he loses that freedom. Man dominates man, and at the center of the *Phenomenology* is the dialectic of master and serf. The relationship of master to serf is one of unfreedom, of domination, but yet a relationship that generates freedom. It is a relationship of oppression, but one that generates equality. For in a despotic society all men are equal, equal before their master, equal in their dependence upon him. But the master too is dependent, dependent on his serfs. This dependence forces him to recognize them as beings on whom he is dependent, as beings with a life of their own. Hence the logic of slavery is such that it leads from the estrangement of men to their mutual recognition. History is a path from unfreedom to freedom. The religion of unfreedom is one that places God outside the world, related to man as the master is to the serf. The recovery of man's true being in a free society is accompanied by an interiorization of religion. Man recognizes the Absolute Spirit in those manifestations of Finite Spirit which are the minds of men. So that in understanding his estrangement so as to overcome it, man passes from art and religion to philosophy. Art uses symbols, but does not claim truth, in the sense that religion does. Religion claims truth, but presents it in symbolic form in the guise of myth. The Christian doctrine of God incarnate in Jesus symbolizes for Hegel the ultimate unity of man and God, of finite and infinite Spirit. But because religion is a product of man's estrangement it objectifies its symbols, it makes God-manhood the attribute of one particular being in one particular time and place, and so becomes superstition. Reason must therefore oppose religion, which falls before its attacks—Hegel is here thinking of eighteenth-century rationalism; but at the critical point philosophy shows the inner truth of what religion has been trying to say. The content of religion is correct. It is its use of images and symbols which distorts the content by an incorrect, but historically necessary form. Hence it is philosophy which finally exhibits the truth of spirit in its historical form of the free society, the society in which self-conscious reason is at work.

The progress of history is then a progress of freedom and a progress in which freedom emerges from slavery. It is this progress which Hegel proceeds to formalize in his dialectic. Slavery, the opposite of freedom, generates freedom which does away with or negates slavery. History passes from one phase to its opposite, for the seeds of the one are contained in the other: and then the third is completed by a synthesis of the two opposite phases, which is possible because of their fundamental unity. Thesis is negated by antithesis, and both are at once united and transcended in the negation of the negation. But if this is the pattern of history, it is the pattern of mind or spirit, and hence the pattern of the universe. For nature itself must be a product of spirit, since mind can envisage it. This, the theme of Hegel's *Logic*, takes abstraction and a falsifying scholasticism to their final point. It is this idealist aspect of Hegel to which attention is commonly directed. But the final scholastic abstractions can never be understood, except as an attempt to systematize the whole of historical and natural knowledge in terms of the concepts of reconciliation with which the younger Hegel had illuminated a certain amount of real history.

Two points remain. How should we account for Hegel's optimism about the outcome of history? Why does he see so clearly the victory of freedom? Part of the answer lies in the attention that the younger Hegel paid to Adam Smith. What impressed him was Adam Smith's version of the common eighteenth-century vision of each individual pursuing his private interest in the economic sphere and in so doing, bringing about the common good, an end which the individual had never envisaged. This suggested to Hegel that self-interest and other evils are overcome in the historical process. But this raises at once a second question. Surely Hegel should have seen that in fact they are not overcome, that rising capitalism did not necessarily produce the common good, but often the misery of many? The answer to this is twofold. First, as Lukacs has pointed out, Hegel is a representative of the bourgeois genius in the period of its greatest optimism. Secondly—and there is perhaps a connection—Hegel's idealism divorces him from the actuality of history. By his idealism I mean his dependence on his own basic concepts and his substitution of a conceptual system for the material reality of nature and history. History becomes for the mature Hegel merely a manifestation of the idea, of reason at work. This confusion of the real and the ideal, of what is and of what in Hegelian terms ought to be, led Hegel to identify the Prussian state of his day with the most complete expression to date of the ideal state of which his system spoke. Hegel's dialectic that spoke of the development of freedom from despotism notoriously became itself an instrument of despotism in the service of the Prussian state.

Nevertheless, a more defensible form of the antithesis between what man is empirically and what he really is and ought to be is fundamental to the core of Hegel's thought; but this distinction between man's essence and man's existence is complicated by Hegel's seeing the ideal incarnate in the real in the Prussia of his day politically and in his own system philosophically. What distorts Hegel's thinking is his refusal to make his thought conform to historical reality. Hegel seeks to deliver man by right thinking, but he claims for thinking a false autonomy. Man as thinker is not autonomous: he belongs to a material world, from which his thinking arises. Hegel forgot what Kierkegaard remembered when Kierkegaard said that the tragedy of the speculative philosopher is that he must turn aside from his place as a spectator of time and eternity in order to sneeze.

Thus Hegel's vision of man incarnates Christian themes: but to religion itself he gives only a temporary role, that of waiting until philosophy shall set forth truth itself. What discredits religion is its use of image and myth; these belong to man's estrangement. In his redeemed state man, in Hegel's view, must conform to a rationality which excludes myth and image. Once more Hegel is realizing Pauline eschatology, with a secular version of the time when we shall put by knowing in a glass darkly and shall instead see face to face.

III.

PHILOSOPHY IN TRANSITION: HEGEL TO FEUERBACH

We all became Feuerbachians.
—F. ENGELS

HEGEL'S MATURE SYSTEM has grave consequences for practice. At the heart of the Hegelian world view is the formula: freedom is the knowledge of necessity; or, as Hegel puts it elsewhere: necessity is blind only insofar as it is not understood. That is, when we understand the laws of our nature and the laws of the universe, they no longer constrain us as they had before we realized their constraining power; but rather we are able to use our knowledge of these laws to serve our own purposes. The law of gravity cannot be broken; but, once apprehended, we can take it into account in our planning, and so are set free from a blind acquiescence to its consequences. To be free then is to understand the laws that necessarily govern nature and society. It is consequently of the first importance to determine the character of these laws. In Hegel's view the outstanding fact about the laws that govern the universe is that they are the expression of the absolute idea, of spirit, of thought. It is the idea, it is thought, which is, in Hegel's phrase, the demiurge of reality. To change reality one must change thought. To change the reality of society one must change the thought of society, and accordingly, to preserve and safeguard society in its present form, one must preserve and safeguard its thought. Thus the battle between political and social conservatives and reformers is essentially a battle of ideas, in which the speculative thinkers, the philosophers, will take the foremost place. This is the consequence which many of Hegel's disciples drew from his philosophy, even though in Hegel's own view the philosopher understands history after the event and not before. But they at once divided into parties of Right and Left on the question of their attitude to political and religious questions. The Right Hegelians stressed Hegel's political conservatism (which was beyond suspicion) and his religious orthodoxy (which was quite suspect although he was officially a Lutheran until his death). They emphasized the Christian ancestry of the absolute idea, and finally in the work of Biedermann, Hegelian philosophy, sprung as it was from

Christian theology, returned to the fold of Lutheran dogmatics. The Left Hegelians, Strauss, the Bauers, Stirner, were liberal in politics and skeptical in religion. They argued that if the absolute idea finds the sum of its manifestations in human thinking, then the absolute idea is nothing but a personification, a theological distortion of human thinking. Hegel was right in seeing human thinking as the crown of reality, but this very fact precludes the existence of anything beyond the human. Religion and theology are mere superstition—in Hegel himself only a façade—and the first task of philosophy is to eliminate them from our thought. It is a further consequence of the Left Hegelian view that if thinking, if opinions are the key to changing the world, then the central political questions are those of academic freedom and of freedom of speech. This contention, together with their attack on religion, brought the Left Hegelians into immediate conflict with the reactionary Prussian governments of the 1830's and 1840's. This opposition to the political *status quo* confirmed their opinion of themselves as political revolutionaries, but it did not change their view that the method of revolution is criticism, that is to say the propagation of the right ideas. Ideas are the source of both the good and the evil in the world. Ideas for the Left Hegelians had a remarkable

[21]

power. Marx satirized their views admirably in the Preface to *The German Ideology*: "Once upon a time an honest fellow had the idea that men were drowned in water only because they were possessed with the idea of gravity. If they were to knock this idea out of their heads, say by stating it to be a superstition, a religious idea, they would be sublimely proof against any danger from water. His whole life long he fought against the illusion of gravity, of whose harmful results all statistics brought him new and manifold evidence. This honest fellow was the type of the new revolutionary philosophers in Germany."

The landmark of the Left Hegelians' criticism of religion was D. F. Strauss's *Life of Jesus*, the first volume of which was published in 1835, the second a year later. Strauss's starting point is the typically Hegelian one that the idea of God-manhood, of humanity as the essential content of the divine, does not depend for its perfection or reality on how far it was in fact realized in the person of Jesus: the perfection and reality of the idea are intrinsic to it as an idea. Historically Jesus was the first to introduce it to the minds of men: therein lies His glory. But the idea is independent of the person: herein lies the idealism of Strauss. The life of Jesus is mythical, and by myth is meant the clothing of religious ideas in historical form.

Strauss proceeds to demythologize the gospel, eliminating the miracles and leaving a Jesus with definite but mistaken expectations of His coming again. "If in any period of His life," writes Strauss, "He held Himself to be a Messiah—and that there was a period when He did so, there can be no doubt—and if He described himself as the Son of Man, He must have expected the coming in the clouds which Daniel had ascribed to the Son of Man." Strauss's view of a historical Jesus was attacked by Bruno Bauer who saw the gospel not as a mythical transformation of the historical Jesus so much as a reflection of the experience of the early Church, and conceived that experience in Hegelian terms. Christianity forces the self-conscious subject from the world by making it aware of itself in opposition to the world. It was the impact of the early Roman Empire that forced this awareness of the individual self-consciousness upon itself by confronting it with powers before which it stood in helpless opposition. But the alienation of the self from the world is not overcome by Christianity, which perpetuates that alienation by giving it a mythological and miraculous form. Once we understand the ways in which the gospel has its historical context in the struggle of the early Church against the Roman Empire, then we can understand both the reasons for

the mythological form of the gospel and also why
such a gospel no longer has contemporary relevance.
So Christianity is now envisaged finally not as a set of
historical facts (whether genuine or not), but as a set
of speculative doctrines in mythological form. To
draw the Christian vision of man's condition back into
the realm of history was the task of Ludwig Feuerbach.

The Young Hegelians had denied the theological
implications of Hegel, but had preserved his abstractions. Reason, thought, the idea, the subject-object
relationship, these are their intellectual currency.
Feuerbach himself was at first a Hegelian, then a Left
Hegelian, and only finally a materialist, or, more accu-
rately, a humanist. For Feuerbach replaced abstract
reason by the concrete reasoning of man. He outlined
his own intellectual history in the aphorism: "God was
my first thought; reason, my second; and man, my
third and last." Where the Hegelians placed an abstract
subject and object, Feuerbach put the concrete I and
Thou. For Feuerbach all thinking is social, and therefore beyond thought there is the thinker, a thinker,
at that, who belongs to a material world in which he
is not alone. Thought is not independent, autonomous.
Thought must conform to two conditions: it must
remain conscious that it is derivative from being out-

side itself, that it pictures an independent world; and, secondly, thought is not a private activity, it is a part of man's intercourse with his fellow men. The first point is made by Feuerbach in his *Theses on the Reform of Philosophy* when he writes: "The true relationship between thought and being may be expressed as follows: being is the subject and thought the predicate. Thought is conditioned by being, not being by thought. Being is conditioned by itself, has its basis in itself." He makes the second point in the words, "The true dialectic is nowise a dialogue of the solitary thinker with himself, it is a dialogue between the I and the Thou." Man, then, is a material being. "Man is what he eats." But equally, man is formed by his relations with other men. "Man as a being sprung from nature is a creature of nature, not a man. Man is the product of man, of culture, of history." But man who thinks is always dependent on man who eats. "If because of hunger, of misery, you have no foodstuff in your body, you likewise have no stuff for morality in your head." This is the basis of Feuerbach's materialism. The world must be encountered in experience, before it can become an object of thought. "Thought is preceded by being; before thinking a quality, you feel it." The Hegelian unity of subject and object is simply man as subject apprehending the world as object. The world as object includes other subjects. The "I" encounters the "Thou." From the subjective point of view this is a spiritual encounter, from the objective a material. "I am a psychological object for myself, but a physiological object for another person."

Thought, then, is a human activity. Its subject matter is being, for, "It is not thought which determines being, but being which determines thought." The form that subject matter takes is determined by the fact that thinking is a social activity, a human activity. "Art, religion, philosophy and science," says Feuerbach, "are only manifestations or revelations of the human essence." What is the human essence? "The human essence can only be found in the unity of man with man." Beyond man in community there is no proper object of knowledge. It is the failure to appreciate this which fosters religious illusions. Religion has no objective content. "Not *Deus sive natura*," wrote Feuerbach in his criticism of Spinoza, "but *aut Deus aut natura*. That is where truth lies." How, then, does religion arise? It arises because men objectify the essence of humanity and distinguish "humanity" from the world of living men. The images of religion are a fantastic projection and distortion of human nature. Feuerbach is a follower of Hegel in seeing Christianity as correct in its content, mistaken in its form. The God of the Christian religion is, for Feuerbach, a vision of humanity. The heart of the Christian religion is contained in the statement, "God is love." The real, but concealed, content of this statement is an affirmation that love is the source of human community. The theological language is a mere disguise. Hence the gospel must be humanized. This is the task undertaken by Feuerbach in his work *The Essence of the Christian Religion*. The error of man is the Hegelian one of objectification: the source of man's error is wrong thinking; the corrective is right thinking. Thought is, for Feuerbach, the most deeply human of all activities. He retains the biblical conception of human nature insofar as he sees freedom in community as the core of that nature, and insofar as he sees that such community must be realized historically. But how the true community of Feuerbach's humanistic version of Christianity is to be realized, Feuerbach does not ask. Both Hegel and Feuerbach are quite frankly attempting to realize Christianity in secular terms; both attempt to rid it of myth in order to do this. This leads both of them to see the path of our redemption as through theoretical reflection. Feuerbach could say that "politics must become our religion," but he thinks of politics as an affair of rival theories. Religion, when it is made concrete by Feuerbach, is usually rather a matter of the more intimate personal relationships. Feuerbach sees that man eats and loves as well as thinks. What he does not see is the wholeness of man who does all these things or the alienation of man in all these activities.

IV.

FROM PHILOSOPHY TO PRACTICE: MARX

Marx's philosophy would necessarily . . . appear
nonsensical except to a person who, I will not say
shared his desire to make the world better by
means of a philosophy, but at least regarded that
desire as a reasonable one.
—R. G. COLLINGWOOD

THE CONCEPTS THAT dominate Marx's thinking are
drawn from Hegel and Feuerbach; the use he makes
of them is his own. His starting point was the
rationalistic Christianity of the Enlightenment, which
came to him from his father and his teachers. Nevertheless, the adolescent Marx seems to have had an un-
common awareness, not only of what he inherited in
the way of belief, but also of the fact that the belief
was inherited, was already formed before he received
it. So that he can write in his school essays not only
the sentence, "Who should not gladly endure sor-
rows, when he knows that through his continuing in
Christ, through his works God is honored?" but also
that other sentence in which Franz Mehring sees the
dawn of Marxism: "Our social relations have to some

extent already commenced before we are in a position to determine them."

As a student, Marx could not escape the influence of Hegel. Indeed, the history of his thought is the history of his criticism, first of Hegel, then of the Left Hegelians, and finally of Feuerbach. His relation to Hegel is unique. It might be claimed that insofar as philosophy was concerned, Marx remained a Hegelian to the last; only he saw that philosophy was not enough. But from the outset he could not escape from Hegel, and in particular from those features of Hegel's thought which were intended to embody the positive content of Christianity. It was the completeness of Hegel's philosophy which first impressed Marx: the final system had a place for everything, and all those philosophical positions which might seem to be possible alternatives to Hegelianism had been shown by Hegel in his *History of Philosophy* to be nothing but incomplete approximations to the Hegelian view. This is as true of philosophies apparently alien to Hegel as it is of those whose likeness is obvious. For if the history of philosophy is a Hegelian dialectic, then the final system will spring not simply from like earlier systems, but from the synthesis of like and unlike. Hence the young Marx complains that no matter where he begins in philosophy, his train of thought ultimately leads him back to Hegel. He tries to innovate, to produce a new logic starting out afresh from Kant and Fichte and "My last sentence was the beginning of the Hegelian system."

At the same time, Marx was conscious of the need for a new point of departure in philosophy. In the letter to his father of November 10, 1837, Marx makes clear that his problem is to find a way through Hegel's idealism, and to do this by discovering the Hegelian idea in things themselves, rather than in abstractions. His first insight came with the realization that the situation of German philosophy after Hegel resembled strikingly the situation of Greek philosophy after Aristotle. Aristotle had produced a complete and systematic philosophy, and he, too, had seen the history of philosophy as a series of approximations to the finality of his own system. Marx's doctoral thesis, which deals in detail with Epicurus' transformation of the atomic theory of Democritus, is in fact part of his study of what happened to Greek philosophy after Aristotle. What happened to Greek philosophy is that it became practical. It turned from speculative metaphysics to ethics. This suggests the solution of Marx's problem. Hegel has in principle completed the task of speculative philosophy. But Hegel's philosophy remains in the realm of speculation, of the ideal. What must be achieved is the realization of the ideal in the world not simply of thought, but of material reality. Hegel's theory must be converted into Marx's practice. This is Marx's problem. But even in his formulation of this problem of how to pass beyond Hegel, Marx remains a Hegelian. For when he sees the Hegelian philosophy as the final synthesis in thought of the ideal, and sets it over against its antithesis, the real material world of the nineteenth century, and then attempts to realize the former in the latter—when Marx does all this—what else is he doing but initiating a new phase of Hegel's own dialectic?

Marx's starting point is the contradiction between Hegel's view of the ideal state and the contemporary Prussian state. His immediate tasks are two: to complete and correct Hegel's view of the ideal, and to discover how it shall be translated into actuality. His conception of the first task is governed by the fact that he agrees with the Left Hegelians in their anti-theological interpretation of Hegel. Marx agreed with Bruno Bauer in seeing the absolute spirit of which Hegel spoke as being in objective content simply the free self-consciousness of men. Later he was to collaborate with Bauer in a work issued anonymously, *The Trumpet of the Last Judgment over Hegel the Atheist and Antichrist.* This brought out the heterodoxy of Hegel by purporting to be from the hand of a pious and alarmed Lutheran, deploring the official sanction given to Hegel and pointing out how the views of the Left Hegelians spring naturally from Hegel. Hence Marx, too, plays his part in drawing the full consequences of Hegel's own thought from Hegel's writings, and in correcting Hegel's political and religious philosophy in Hegelian terms.

It is thus possible for Hegelianism to take up one of two differing and opposed attitudes. These are outlined in some notes for Marx's thesis and in a paper entitled "Key Points in the Development of Philosophy." The completion of thought in theoretical terms by both Aristotle and Hegel calls for an awakening of will to realize thought in the world of actual being. In this situation Marx's contemporaries can be divided into two parties. The one seeing the gap between theory and reality seeks to bridge it by changing reality so that the world will conform to the ideal of theory. The other seeks instead to adapt theory to reality, changing philosophy so as to make it conform to the actual world in which they live. Paradoxically, the result of each attempt is the opposite of what was intended. The first party, which Marx calls the "liberals," tries to use philosophy to change the world. But in this light philosophy ceases to be mere theory and becomes instead a weapon, an instrument of practice. This changes its whole character. Seeking to transform the world, the "liberals" transform philosophy. Their opponents attempt to change philosophy to conform to the actual world. But in fact this leads them to uphold the world as it is, the *status quo*. Seeking to transform philosophy, the opponents of liberalism make an impact upon the world. Thus, if we set out to change the world in a progressive sense, we must be prepared in so doing to transform our philosophy into an instrument of our action. The first steps in doing this will be to understand the implications of our theory and then to understand why theory *qua* theory needs to be transformed in order to be an instrument of practical activity. This understanding Marx acquired in his activities first as contributor and then as editor of the *Rheinische Zeitung*.

In this capacity the contradiction between the ideal state of which Hegel spoke and the Prussian state of his day was fully brought home to him. The ideal state was to be the expression of the free society of men. But the Prussian state exercised a censorship of the press in the interest of some views and to the detriment of others. In other words, the state only expressed the views and interests of some elements in society. The state and society in practice are not one, but the state is an instrument that governs and represses society. Hence Hegel was profoundly mistaken in seeing the Prussian state as an expression of the free society. This error of Hegel's rests on a misunderstanding of the proper relationship of society and the state. Hegel's idealism leads him to see the state as forming society, for the state embodies a rational will which imposes its forms upon society. Marx, in contrast, insists that society exists prior to the state, that the state grows out of society. Hence, for Hegel, political and social institutions are to be explained in terms of the degree of rationality that they manifest, and political and social change is a development in logic. "The transition," says Marx, commenting on Hegel's *Philosophy of Mind* in 1843, "is not traced from the special nature of the family, the special nature of the state, and so forth, but from the general relation of necessity and freedom." For Marx, the state is the concrete historical growth, with a social background. Its development is to be understood in particular, not in general terms.

If Marx rejects Hegel's view of the relation of the state to society, he rejects even more summarily two corollaries which Hegel had drawn from it. The first is Hegel's argument that every people has the government it deserves. For, in Hegel's eyes, the state is society become rational, and therefore the form of the state represents the form given to the state by society become politically conscious. Hence the state cannot but represent the true wishes of society, for its form is the manifestation of these wishes. This view for Marx is falsified by actual history. Political constitutions do not, as an observed fact, change with the changing needs and desires of society. This leads Marx to criticize Hegel's support of constitutional monarchy as the ideal form of constitution. Hegel's view of the state leads him to hold that the state, as the consciousness of society, expresses the will of society; there is, then, a will of society which is one will. But that will must be embodied in an actual subject, that is, in one man. There must therefore be one man in whom the ruling will of the state is embodied—the monarch. Hence Hegel concludes that monarchy is the ideal form of society. Marx attacks both the sophistry of this argument and its political conclusions. He argues that the will of the people is only expressed in the state when people and state coincide, when the sovereignty is shared by every citizen in a state where to be a man is to be a citizen. Citizenship is to be a quality of man. Hence democracy is the ideal form of state. Marx traces Hegel's error to its root in Hegel's concentration not on men but on abstractions which he treats as qualities not of mankind, but of the idea.

In the light of this ideal of democracy, Marx makes short work of Hegel's detailed defense of the existing Prussian constitution. Throughout his analysis of Hegel he draws attention to the way in which Hegel sees the constitution as exemplifying abstract general principles and concepts, and the part of man in political life as being merely to represent the same principles and concepts. In contrast, Marx emphasizes the fact that politics is a human activity and that the ultimate reality is that of man. The failure of Hegelian political theory and of Prussian political practice is a failure to accord with the true nature of man in society. The proper form of human life is democracy. In all this Marx reveals the profound influence of Feuerbach. He inherits from Feuerbach a doctrine of essential human nature as being revealed in society, and it is this that he uses to modify Hegel. At the same time, the reality of the Prussian state brings out for him the difference between what man in society ought to be—the democratic citizen—and what man under the Prussian despotism actually is. Whence this contradiction? The beginning of an answer to this question Marx found through two encounters, the first with Moses Hess, who helped to introduce him to an earlier socialism, the second with Friedrich Engels, who introduced him to the realities of developed industrial capitalism in England. Marx had met Hess as early as 1841. Engels met Marx in Cologne in 1842 on his way to Manchester, where he saw the textile industry from the inside. Before he left Cologne he had himself come under the influence of Hess, but it was not until two years later that his partnership with Marx commenced. Nevertheless, during his stay in England he had already contributed vivid accounts of English industrial life to the left-wing press on the Continent.

The earlier socialism was that which Marx was to christen Utopian. Its exponents were Owen, Fourier, and Saint-Simon. All attacked existing society. All had an ideal of what society should be. All failed to prescribe an effective means for converting the one into the other. What they did for Marx was to give precision to his vision of the good society. Saint-Simon in particular was concerned with what he called "the present anarchy of production" and had already begun the criticism of the unplanned enterprise of capitalism. He could write of the future state that he envisaged that "production will not be directed by isolated enterprises independent of each other and ignorant of the needs of the people; this task will be entrusted to a specific social institution." He could also write that "the individual right of property can be based only on the common and general utility of the exercise of this right—a utility which may vary with the period." Thus a socialism of this kind helped to direct Marx's attention to the property relations within any given society as well as to its political forms. The importance of property relations, however, was brought out more strikingly by contemporary industrial capitalism and by the living conditions it created. Engels sums up the state of the working classes in the English cities as follows:

> The great towns are chiefly inhabited by working people, since in the best case there is one bourgeois for two workers, often for three, here and there for four; these workers have no property whatsoever of their own, and live wholly upon wages, which usually go from hand to mouth. Society, composed wholly of atoms, does not trouble itself about them; leaves them to care for themselves and their families, yet supplies them no means of doing this in an efficient and permanent manner. Every workingman, even the best, is therefore constantly exposed to loss of work and food, that is, to death by starvation, and many perish in this way. The dwellings of the workers are everywhere

badly planned, badly built, and kept in the worst condition, badly ventilated, damp and unwholesome. The inhabitants are confined to the smallest possible space, and at least one family usually sleeps in each room. The interior arrangement of the dwellings is poverty-stricken in various degrees, down to the utter absence of even the most necessary furniture. The clothing of the workers, too, is generally scanty, and that of great multitudes is in rags. The food is, in general, bad; often almost unfit for use, and in many cases, at least at times, insufficient in quantity, so that, in extreme cases, death by starvation results. Thus the working class of the great cities offers a graduated scale of conditions in life, in the best cases a temporarily endurable existence for hard work and good wages, good and endurable, that is, from the workers' standpoint; in the worst cases, bitter want, reaching even homelessness and death by starvation. The average is much nearer the worst case than the best.

This description dates from 1844.

Thus Marx is faced with a stark antithesis; on the one hand, Hegel and Feuerbach have enabled him to understand the inescapability of the goal of human freedom for contemporary men; on the other hand, he cannot but see the reality of work, degradation, and suffering which is the lot of the majority. The two questions that arise for him can only be: How did this contrast arise? And, how is it to be ended? They are questions that demand action, and hence the transformation of philosophy into an instrument of practice becomes even more urgent. But in order to understand the antithesis of social and economic life Marx was thrown back on an intense study of political economy, and his new outlook on society led in turn to a new criticism of Feuerbach and Hegel.

What comes to the fore in Marx's thought is the importance of the political. Because the actual state is not fully a realization of the true form of the state, we can understand from the present political forms the immediate course of society. "As religion is the index of man's theoretical struggles, so is the political state that of his practical struggles." In the course of a discussion with Bruno Bauer over the political rights of the Jews, Marx brings out both the benefits of political equality and its limitations. The state may grant men equal political rights, but it ignores the basic inequalities of birth, occupation, and property which render men in practice unequal. Thus man as a member of the state, a society of equality, is in contradiction with himself as a member of civil society, a society of inequality. What the granting of political rights to religious minorities, such as the Jews, does is to make religious belief no longer a concern of the state, but instead a private matter. The state is emancipated from religion. But man in such a state is still not fully emancipated, for the power that men achieve with the granting of political rights is severely limited by the power wielded within society by those with property over against those lacking it. The basic inequalities due to property must be eliminated if the state is to be a society of free and equal members. Marx quotes from the sixteenth-century Anabaptist Thomas Münzer: "All things have become property, the fish in the water, the birds of the air and all that groweth upon the Earth—the creatures must become free." Political emancipation is something, but it is not enough.

What the state must do is to exemplify the free society of free men in concrete form. To do this it must be capable of dealing with human realities. Marx's criticism of Feuerbach here is that while Feuerbach recognizes that the objects of religious belief are a fantastic projection of human needs and ideals, he never accounts for the rise of religion in terms of those needs and aspirations. Marx is quite clear about what religion is. In his "Introduction to a Critique of Hegel's Philosophy of Right" he calls it "the sigh of the oppressed creature." "It is the opium of the people," he says in the next sentence. Feuerbach explains it as springing from man: but Feuerbach's view of man is too abstract: "Man is no abstract being, squatting somewhere beyond the world. Man is the human world, the state, society." But the religious vision and its transmutations in German philosophy spring out of society: in order that they shall be fulfilled and realized in the accomplishment of the good society that they envisage, they themselves will have to make way for a more radical philosophy, a philosophy of social practice. But society is divided: this is indeed a sign of the ills that beset it. Who then is to change it? The clue to Marx's later answer is already given in his description of the workingmen whom he met in Paris in 1844: "Among these people the brotherhood of man is no phrase, but truth and human nobility shine from their labor-hardened forms."

V.

MARX'S ACCOUNT OF HISTORY

> We have now followed the proletariat of the British Islands through all branches of its activity, and found it everywhere living in want and misery under totally inhuman conditions. We have seen discontent arise with the rise of the proletariat, grow, develop and organize; we have seen open bloodless and bloody battles of the proletariat against the bourgeoisie. We have investigated the principles according to which the fate, the hopes and fears of the proletariat are determined, and we have found that there is no prospect of improvement in their condition.
>
> —F. ENGELS (*in 1844*)

BY 1844, Marx had to hand all the materials that he needed for his philosophy of history. The first attempt at it is to be found in the essay of that year, entitled "National Economy and Philosophy." His approach to the fundamental themes of this essay was through his reading of David Ricardo and the enlightenment he drew from Ricardo's formulation of the labor theory of value. What he learned from Ricardo was that the injustice of society toward the common people rests on a distribution of property that is only possible because the common people, by their labor, have created that property in the first instance. He uses this view of the centrality of labor to elucidate the truth hidden in various Hegelian and Feuerbachian doctrines. The form of the argument needs disentangling, for the manuscript is full of repetitions, abrupt breakings off, asides, and the like. The essay is in three parts, of which the first is on the alienation of labor, the second on the nature of private property, while the third has sections on the relation of private property to labor, on the transition from private property to communism, on the division of labor and the role of money, and, finally, a series of notes on Hegel's *Phenomenology of Mind*. The main course of the argument in the first manuscript was as follows.

In his Preface Marx had said that it was Feuerbach who had made a critical economics possible: his own starting point is typically Feuerbachian. Traditionally, national economy (as it was called in Germany—the English term is political economy—has assumed the existence of private property and has based its observations on the property relations deriving therefrom. What now has to be done is to pierce through that assumption to the fundamental realities of work, of labor. Basic to all is the objective existence of nature—here Marx breaks through the Hegelian insistence that nature itself is merely a product of spirit. "The worker cannot produce without nature, without the world of sense. It is the material through which his labor realizes itself, in which it is active, from which and by means of which it is productive." Work, labor is the basis of production. Hence, not only are the products of labor commodities to be bought and sold, but labor itself, the means of production, becomes a commodity to be bought and sold for wages. "Labor produces not only commodities: it produces itself and the worker as a commodity." This process Marx interprets in Hegelian terms. When man as worker becomes himself a commodity, he is fundamentally alienated, estranged from himself. In the form of labor, man sees himself as a commodity, as an object. Hence, as labor he objectifies, externalizes his own existence. A consequence of this is that life becomes not something he enjoys as a part of his essential humanity, but rather merely an opportunity to earn a living, a bare physical subsistence that will enable him to go on working. Man, objectifying his life in the form of labor, is alienated from a truly human life. "Then, for the first time," writes Marx, "work, the activity of life, the productive life, appears to man only as a means to supply a need, the need of maintaining physical existence." Nevertheless, this estrangement makes man human. In seeing his life as an object, a commodity—labor—man becomes a reflective and not merely an instinctive being. "The animal is immediately at one with its own act of living. It is not differentiated from itself. It is itself. Man makes his very act of living an object of his will and consciousness."

Thus to be human is to be estranged. But when man becomes a being divided against himself, able to envisage himself as a commodity, he breaks the community of man with man. For one man can buy and sell another, in the form of buying and selling his labor. One immediate consequence of the fact that man is estranged from the product of his work (that is, from the commodities which his labor has created, which belong not to him, but to those who bought his labor, that is, himself, in the first place), from the act of being, from his own essential nature, is the estrangement of man from man. When man stands over against himself, other men stand over against him also. What goes for the relation of man to his labor, to the product of his labor and to himself, is true also of the relation of man to other men, and so to the labor and to the objective form of the labor of other men.

[48]

"In short, the estrangement of man from his own essential being means that a man is estranged from others, just as each is estranged from essential humanity." A consequence of this is that man creates a world in which he is a stranger, a world dominated by economic powers that he has created, but that he does not recognize as his own. Because of this lack of recognition, he envisages the powers that rule his life under strange and terrible forms. He sees himself as powerless, and with the power that is really his but that he has given over to external forces, he endows the being that seems to him to rule the world. In other words, he creates the gods. Earlier, Marx had remarked on the parallel between the world created in objectifying labor by making it a commodity, and the world created in objectifying human powers by making them gods. "The more the worker labors, the more powerful becomes the estranged, objectified world that he creates over against himself and the poorer becomes his own inner world, and the less he belongs to himself. It is the same in religion. The more man places in God, the less he retains in himself." But the creation of gods as the masters of men is untruth. The truth is that man, in creating the images of the gods, has enslaved man. "Not gods, not nature, only man himself can be this estranged power over man."

We began with nature and man. Man by his work first creates commodities, then becomes himself a commodity. Attempting to envisage the world that he has made, he creates a universe of strange forces which overcome man from outside, a world of property relationships, that is, of the ownership of commodities and therefore of human life and labor, which divides man and the society of men from within. Thus the estrangement of man gives rise to divisions between man at every level. "Therefore," says Marx, for instance, "the religious self-estrangement appears necessarily in the relation of laity to priests." Labor is the root of all, but private property the final result. "National economy begins with labor as the true soul of production and nevertheless gives labor nothing and private property everything." The logic of this process is Hegel's logic of alienation and of objectification. But its history has yet to be written, and so the first manuscript culminates in the questions: "How has man come to externalize, to be estranged from his labor? How is this estrangement grounded in the essential course of human development?"

The essential antagonism of society is that between worker and capitalist. Adam Smith had given the reasons why the capitalist must always benefit in any struggle between workers and capitalists, and

Marx had already in an earlier note on Adam Smith refuted his contention that wages would rise as a result of competition between capitalists. "The number of laborers is now in all industrial countries above the demand, and can daily be recruited from the workless proletariat, to which it, in turn, daily yields recruits." Whenever the capitalist loses, the worker loses too, for his wages, the price paid for his labor, are determined by the price at which the capitalist can sell his finished product. Whenever the capitalist gains, his increased profits enable him to replace the worker by machinery; and at the same time the division of labor means that the worker's specialized skills restrict his range of employment, so that the gain of the capitalist does not imply any consequent gain on the part of the worker. But this is not all. What the capitalist has to gain or lose is capital. What the worker has to sell for more or less is his labor, that is, himself and his chance of a livelihood. Hence it is the worker's personality, his chance of a properly human life that is destroyed by his loss. In this the economic system is not interested. The worker owning only his labor is, in the present system, nothing else than his labor, a mere commodity, no longer a person, but a thing.

Furthermore, through investment of profits, the capitalist becomes also the landowner. Land itself becomes a commodity, and the tenant becomes a laborer. The expansion of capitalism is all-inclusive. All social relationships are reduced to the essential relation of capitalist and worker, employer and employed. But whence the original source of this capital that enslaves society? Capital is nothing else than accumulated wealth, wealth nothing other than the fruit of labor. Hence Marx's vivid equation at the end of the second manuscript: "Capital = accumulated labor = labor." Capital is labor in disguise. It is the object that the alienation of labor, of work, creates. For labor is alienated in that it has become not a means to a truly human existence, in which the non-human—nature—is made into the image of man by means of art and of science, but is rather now an end in itself, and has thus created an existence for man which is non-human, in which the labor of man creates the power of capital, which destroys all human fruits of man's labor.

Thus it is of the nature of capitalist society to deprive more and more men of an essentially human life. Once again we may return to Marx's earlier annotation of the political economists where he writes: "So it transpires (i) that there is no question of any national or human interest but only of net revenue, profit, rent, that this is the ultimate purpose of a nation, (ii) that a human life has of itself no value, (iii) that the value of the working class is limited to the necessary cost of production." In *National Economy and Philosophy* Marx proceeds to examine what political economy and the earlier socialist writers, respectively, have made of the process whereby man is dehumanized in the creation of the proletariat. Political economy has never quite pierced through the veil of objectified forms in which society conceals the realities of the productive process. It resembles religion in treating as objects what are in fact parts of man's estranged being. Thus it is labor that creates wealth and value, but value is objectified in the form of exchange value and hence in the symbolic form of money. The mercantilists were the fetish-worshipers, the Catholics of political economy who treated money as the real incarnation of value. Adam Smith is like Luther in that he translates symbol into reality, money into labor. But Adam Smith always sees value in the context of a society of private property where labor has its own price, and in the person of the laborer, who owns only his labor, which is itself excluded from private property. The socialist writers similarly have been deceived by outward forms. Proudhon with the slogan, "property is theft," wants to reform the system by abolishing private property, without understanding the social realities which private property represents. Saint-Simon sees labor as the source of society's wealth, but wants to preserve the present industrial system and merely improve the lot of the laborer within it.

Then comes what Marx calls "crude communism." This is really the final expression of the present society. For private property in the form of capital so dominates and overawes present society that the "crude communist" concerns himself with nothing but its abolition. Capitalism denies private property to most, crude communism will deny it to all. Capitalism denied a truly human life to most, crude communism will deny it to all. In Hegelian terms this communism is the negation of the system of private property. But being such a negation it is, in Hegelian terms, necessarily one-sided. It, too, must be negated. A society in which none can achieve true humanity must be replaced by a society in which all can achieve it. This is socialist society. It is to be a society of true communists in which the needs that are satisfied will not be the demands of an economic system, but the needs of man. The values of this society will be human values. Men will deal with other men, neither as with capitalists nor as with proletarians, but as with men. The religion of crude communism is atheism, the negation of the religion of estranged humanity.

[54]

But such atheism is merely negative. Its positive side is philanthropy, the love of men. The philanthropy of atheism is merely abstract; human values have replaced divine values only insofar as they have destroyed the divine. In socialist society human values are themselves fulfilled and the divine is not denied—it has disappeared. Nature is fully realized in man, man in nature. "Here first does his natural existence coincide with his human existence, and nature exist for men. This society is the realized unity in their essential being of men with nature, the true resurrection of nature, the realized naturalism of men, the realized humanism of nature." Nature realizes its human possibilities, man his natural. But the path to a truly human society is through the complete inhumanity of a wholly proletarianized society. That is the way to which history points.

The next part of Marx's work deals with "Need, Production and the Division of Labor," and the following part with "Money." Under the rule of private property, human needs can only be satisfied by selling human labor. But labor has been reduced to the point where the laborer has only his labor, that is himself, to sell, and consequently can only afford to satisfy a few basic needs. The division of labor increases the wealth of society, but renders a man's work still less the free expression of his personality, still more what the economic system demands of him. The consequence is that what ought to be the means of his existence—money—is made into the end; and consequently it is money, the abstract form of man's estrangement, which rules society. Marx quotes Shakespeare in *Timon of Athens:*

Gold? Yellow, glittering, precious gold? No, Gods,
I am no idle votarist. . . .
Thus much of this will make black, white; foul, fair;
Wrong, right; base, noble; old, young; coward, valiant.

It is gold which rules human society. But in a society where man mattered as man, love as love, and art and science as humanizing forces—in such a society, money would count for nothing.

So far, Marx has used Hegelian concepts to elucidate the life of man. Now he turns his analysis back to see Hegelian philosophy itself as part of that life. Political economy placed the essential reality of man outside man; this reality was the victim of false objectification. For political economy the essential reality was money. Philosophy falls into the same error: it, too, objectifies essential human reality and places it outside man. For philosophy, essential reality resides in logic; logic plays the role in philosophy that money plays in political economy. Marx calls logic "the money of the mind." The achievement of Hegel in Marx's eyes was to "see history as a process in which man is estranged from himself, exteriorizes himself and his work, and then finally comes to his own once more." The error of Hegel is to see this as a history not of men, but of abstractions. Hence Hegelian philosophy is itself a false objectification, a substitution of appearance for reality. It, too, belongs to man's estrangement. "The human essence, man, is for Hegel simply self-consciousness. All the estrangement of essential humanity is therefore nothing but the estrangement of self-consciousness. The estrangement of self-consciousness is nothing but an expression reflecting in the forms of knowledge and thought the real estrangement of man's true being." The earlier sections of the essay have enabled us to see estrangement of thought as merely an expression of man's fundamental estrangement. The achievement of Marx here is to have given historical form to a concrete view of what man in society ought to be, of what he is, and of how his estrangement from his own true being comes about.

Having elaborated the philosophy of history implicit in *National Economy and Philosophy*, Marx went on in *The Holy Family*, *The German Ideology*, and *The Poverty of Philosophy* to estimate the thought of the Left Hegelians and Proudhon as merely an expression of the ideology of the middle classes of the 1840's. But if all views are mere expressions of phases of historical process, will not Marx's own view be simply one more such expression? The answer to this is both yes and no. Marx would never have denied the historical conditioning of his views. But at the same time, the proletariat is in a special position where contemporary reality in all its harshness is forced on it, while the middle classes are protected by their favored economic position. So that the proletarian and the thinker who stands beside him will necessarily be able to see further into history. The difference between bourgeois and proletarian is well put by Marx in *The Holy Family*: "The possessing class and the class of the proletariat represent the same human self-estrangement. But the former is comfortable in this self-estrangement and finds therein its own confirmation, knows that this self-estrangement is its own power, and possesses in it the semblance of a human existence. The latter feels itself annihilated in this self-estrangement, sees in it its impotence and the reality of an inhuman existence." The possessing classes are comforted by a semblance; the dispossessed have nothing but reality.

At the same time, Marx, in a new criticism of

Feuerbach, provides a new criterion for the truth of any given philosophy of history. In his Second Thesis on Feuerbach he writes: "The question whether objective truth is an attribute of human thought is not a theoretical but a practical question. Man must prove the truth, i.e., the reality and power, the 'this-sidedness' of his thinking in practice. The dispute over the reality or non-reality of thinking that is isolated from practice is a purely scholastic question." Truth resides not in contemplation but in action. A true philosophy is one that enables us to change reality. Marx here is making several points. First, such truth as we possess is the record not of passive observation of the world, but of active discovery. Second, in changing the world should we start with transforming ourselves and mankind—a change of heart is the phrase often used—or should we begin with transforming circumstances? Marx's answer is that we cannot do the one without doing the other. To acquire a true philosophy is, of course, part of the transformation of oneself: this truth itself is only to be acquired in practice. "The coincidence of the changing of human activity or self-changing can only be comprehended and rationally understood as revolutionary practice." It is only those who are engaged in changing the world who can hope to see the world rightly. The failure of

Feuerbach lies in the inactivity of his philosophy—hence in his abstract view of man. "Feuerbach resolves the essence of religion into the essence of man. But the essence of man is no abstraction inherent in each separate individual. In its reality it is the ensemble of social relations." The failure to realize this led philosophy into the mystifications of religion: the way out of such mystifications is a practice that will abolish their social basis. "All social life is essentially practical. All the mysteries which urge theory into mysticism find their rational solution in human practice and in the comprehension of this practice." Thus practice leads one beyond political truth to social truth. "The standpoint of the old type of materialism is civil society, the standpoint of the new materialism is human society or social humanity." So the Theses on Feuerbach are brought to their pregnant conclusion: "The philosophers have only interpreted the world differently; the point is to change it."

It is this conception of truth that enables Marx both to affirm a historical relativism concerning all philosophies and also to deny that his own philosophy is merely a product of the time, since it is in Marx's own thought that philosophy has for the first time become conscious of its historical basis in seeking to transform that basis and has therefore passed beyond the limitations of earlier philosophy. Thus Marx is able to evaluate his contemporaries from his own new standpoint. His inquiry is delimited by his initial criticism: "It has not occurred to any one of the philosophers to inquire into the connection of German philosophy with German reality, the relation of their criticism to their own material surroundings." This leads Marx to an account of these surroundings, of their history, and of the way in which material surroundings give rise to human consciousness and human philosophies. The following account by Marx and Engels in *The German Ideology* is the first statement of historical materialism:

"The way in which men produce their means of subsistence depends first of all on the nature of the actual means they find in existence and have to reproduce. This mode of production must not be considered simply as being the reproduction of the physical existence of the individuals. Rather it is a definite form of activity of these individuals, a definite form of expressing their life, a definite mode of life on their part. As individuals express their life, so they are. What they are, therefore, coincides with their production, both with what they produce and with how they produce. The nature of individuals thus depends on the material conditions determining their production."

History is, then, essentially the history of changing means of production. In the beginning there is simply the community of men, producing to satisfy their basic needs of food and shelter, discovering, as they satisfy the needs, new needs which in turn demand satisfaction, living together in families, and working together as need demands. The bonds between them are the social bonds of material need and of language. In its earliest simplicity man is still largely animal in his social life. But then the division of labor intervenes to play the part that the Fall plays in Christian theology. The division of labor creates the first real cleavages in society, for it makes of each individual a hunter, a fisherman, a shepherd and so on, who, to maintain his livelihood, must fulfill the demands that the community makes upon his calling rather than the demands of his own nature. Hence we find for the first time a clash between the interest of the individual and that of the community: it is the latter interest which takes political form in the state, an instrument for the coercion of the individual. At the same time, the division of labor means that each individual appropriates the fruits of his own labor and then proceeds to exchange the greater part of them for the goods created by the labor of others. So the division of labor brings with it private property and the problem of exchange values. The system of production and exchange thus created is not of course a voluntary association; it is the natural outcome of the attempt by man to satisfy his needs. But since society is not a voluntary association, it necessarily appears to the individual as an alien power. "The social power, i.e., the multiplied productive force, which arises through the co-operation of different individuals as it is determined within the division of labor, appears to these individuals, since their co-operation is not voluntary but natural, not as their own united power but as an alien force existing outside them, of the origin and end of which they are ignorant, which they thus cannot control, which on the contrary passes through a peculiar series of phases and stays independent of the will and the action of man, nay even being the prime governor of them." The abolition of society as a force opposed to the individual's interest is possible only on two conditions: the vast mass of the people must become propertyless and the productivity of society must reach a level where the needs of all can easily be satisfied. Then it will be possible to fashion a society not based upon the division of labor and therefore upon conflicting social interests.

This possibility opens to man as the climax of a history which is the history of class conflict springing from the division of labor. The history of ideas, of philosophy, is only a part of this greater history. For the very fact that thinking should be the primary occupation of some, the very conception of the professional thinker, is one that results from the basic division of labor between those whose work is primarily mental and those whose work is primarily physical. The thinker always belongs to some one social class. "The ideas of the ruling class are in every epoch the ruling ideas; i.e., the class which is the ruling material force of society is at the same time its ruling intellectual force." The succession of ruling classes is determined by economic changes, which themselves spring from the division of labor. "The greatest division of material and mental labor is the separation of town and country. . . . The existence of the town implies, at the same time, the necessity of administration, police, taxes, etc.; in short, of the municipality, and thus of politics in general. . . . The antagonism of town and country can only exist as a result of private property. It is the most crass expression of the subjection of the individual under the division of labor, under a definite activity forced upon him—a subjection which makes one man into a restricted town animal, the other into a restricted country animal, and daily creates anew the conflict between their interests. The separation of town and country can also be understood as the separation of capital and landed property, as the beginning of the existence and development of capital independent of landed property—the beginning of property having its basis only in labor and exchange."

The modern town dates from the Middle Ages and was created by freed serfs, whose initial capital was simply the tools of their trade, and who had at their disposal no labor other than their own. Competition in the various trades and the need of protection from other trades and from the land-owning powers led to the organization of municipalities and of guilds within municipalities. Later the serfs who entered the life of the town found an established economic system in which, if skilled, they could take their place. If unskilled, they became day laborers, an unorganized rabble. Among the guilds the division of labor was natural as between various guilds and as between individual members of the guilds. "Every workman had to be versed in a whole round of tasks, had to be able to make everything that was made with his tools. . . . Thus there is found with medieval craftsmen an interest in their special work and in proficiency in it, which was capable of rising to a narrow artistic sense." The capital of these workmen was still simply a house, tools, and the goodwill of their trade; and such capital descended simply from father to son.

At this point came the next great division of labor, that between production and commerce. The capital of those engaged in commerce is, of course, monetary and their ability to trade is not confined to a particular neighborhood. Consequently, there is a far greater exchange of goods between different neighborhoods, and as a further consequence there is specialization of production not simply within towns, but between towns. One town will now become the center for this trade or manufacture, another for that. This is only made possible by commerce becoming independent of production. This new interdependence of the towns in the Middle Ages led their ruling class, the burghers, increasingly to assert their common interests against the landed powers of the still feudal countryside. Thus the bourgeoisie as a class was created. "The bourgeoisie itself, with its conditions, develops only gradually, splits according to the division of labor into various fractions and finally absorbs all earlier possessing classes (while it develops the majority of the earlier non-possessing, and a part of the earlier possessing class into a new class, the proletariat) in the measure to which all earlier property is transformed into industrial or commercial capital." The new development of manufacture outside the guild system led to a vast increase in trade, to a new mobility of capital, to new relationships between worker and employer. The mercantilist period of expansion and competition led, in turn, to a new advance—that into large-scale industry. "The concentration of trade and manufacture in one country, England, developing irresistibly in the seventeenth century, gradually created for this country a relative world market, and thus a demand for the manufactured products of this country, which could no longer be met by the industrial productive forces hitherto existing. This demand, outgrowing the productive forces, was the motive power which, by producing big industry—the application of elemental forces to industrial ends, machinery and the most complex division of labor—called into existence the third period of private ownership since the Middle Ages." The effects of large-scale industry are admirably summarized: "Big industry universalized competition in spite of these protective measures . . . established means of communication and the modern world market subordinated trade to itself, transformed all capital into industrial capital, and thus produced the rapid circulation (the financial system is perfected) and the centralization of the various forms of capital. . . . It made natural science subservient to capital and took from the division of labor the last semblance of its natural character. It destroyed natural growth in general, as far as this is possible while labor exists, and resolved all natural relationships into money relationships. . . . And finally, while the bourgeoisie of each nation still retained separate national interests, big industry created a class, which in all nations has the same interest and with which nationality is already dead; a class which is really rid of all the old world and at the same time stands pitted against it. For the worker it makes not only the relation to the capitalist, but labor itself, unbearable."

Marx then outlines the way in which law and politics have a form determined by the historical development of property relations. Then comes his final conclusion: the domination of individuals by the forces of production is nearing its close. For since the bourgeoisie has left only two classes in the struggle, the possessors and the dispossessed, the victory of the latter will make an end not simply to the rule of one class, but to class rule as such. At the same time the bourgeoisie has created productive forces great enough to free man from the bondage imposed upon him by the division of labor. Marx comes to the revolutionary conclusion that every previous servile class has been able to free itself within the social organization and to view its earlier servitude as merely an essential condition of its rise. "For the proletarians on the other hand, the condition of their existence, labor, and with it all the conditions of existence governing modern society, have become something accidental, something over which they, as separate individuals, have no control, and over which no social organization can give them control. The contradiction between the individuality of each separate proletarian and labor, the condition of life forced upon him, becomes evident to him himself, for he is sacrificed from youth upwards, and, within his own class, has no chance of arriving at the conditions that would place him in the other class. Thus, while the refugee serfs only wished to be free to develop and assert those conditions of existence which were already there, and hence, in the end, only arrived at free labor, the proletarians, if they are to assert themselves as individuals, will have to abolish the very conditions of their existence hitherto (which has, moreover, been that of all society up to the present)—namely, labor. Thus they find themselves directly opposed to the form in which, hitherto, individuals have given themselves collective expression, that is, the State. In order, therefore, to assert themselves as individuals, they must overthrow the State."

It is as a natural sequel to this that we come to the first mature statement of Marx's views in which the movement toward social science has expelled much of the earlier Hegelian terminology. That statement is the *Communist Manifesto* of 1848. Its authors were Marx and Engels, but Engels himself best summarized its essential content and attributed that content to Marx in his preface to the English edition of 1888:

The *Manifesto* being our joint production, I consider myself bound to state that the fundamental proposition which forms its nucleus, belongs to Marx. That proposition is: That in every historical epoch, the prevailing mode of economic production and exchange, and the social organization necessarily following from it, form the basis upon which is built up, and from which alone can be explained, the political and intellectual history of that epoch; that consequently the whole history of mankind (since the dissolution of primitive tribal society, holding land in common ownership) has been a history of class struggles, contests between exploiting and exploited, ruling and oppressed classes; that the history of these class struggles forms a series of evolutions in which, nowadays, a stage has been reached where the exploited and op-

pressed class—the proletariat—cannot attain its emancipation from the sway of the exploiting and ruling
class—the bourgeoisie—without at the same time, and
once and for all, emancipating society at large from
all exploitation, oppression, class distinction and class
struggles.

Engels comments: "This proposition . . . in my
opinion, is destined to do for history what Darwin's
theory has done for biology. . . ." At the same time
the *Manifesto* is a call to action: that is as clear from
its vivid opening words, "A spectre is haunting Europe—the spectre of Communism," as from its mag-
nificent close, "The Communists disdain to conceal
their views and aims. They openly declare that their
ends can be attained only by the forcible overthrow
of all existing social conditions. Let the ruling classes
tremble at a communist revolution. In it the proletarians have nothing to lose but their chains. They
have a world to win. Working men of all countries,
unite!" There is thus embedded in this work the un-
easy alliance of science and prophetic harangue that
has already confronted us.

The *Manifesto* begins with outlining the history of society. It contains a fine recognition of the
achievements of the bourgeoisie as well as a denuncia-
tion of the evils of bourgeois society. The "bour-

geoisie . . . has been the first to show what man's activity can bring about. It has accomplished wonders far surpassing Egyptian pyramids, Roman aqueducts and Gothic cathedrals. . . . The bourgeoisie . . . draws all nations . . . into civilization. It has created enormous cities . . . and thus rescued a considerable part of the population from the idiocy of rural life. . . . The bourgeoisie, during its rule of scarcely one hundred years, has created more massive and more colossal productive forces than have all preceding generations together." But this panegyric is only a preparation for the proclamation that the final outcome of the history of the bourgeoisie must be its downfall. "The essential condition for the existence and for the sway of the bourgeois class is the accumulation of wealth in the hands of private individuals, the formation and augmentation of capital; the condition for capital is wage labor. Wage labor rests exclusively on competition between the laborers. The advance of industry, whose involuntary promoter is the bourgeoisie, replaces the isolation of the laborers, due to competition, by their revolutionary combination, due to association. The development of modern industry, therefore, cuts from under the feet of the bourgeoisie the very foundation on which it produces and appropriates products. What the bourgeoisie therefore produces, above all, are its own gravediggers. Its fall and the victory of the proletariat are equally inevitable."

The *Manifesto* then proceeds to define the position of the Communist Party. Marx and Engels had indeed been commissioned by the Communist League to produce the *Manifesto* as their program. The Communist League was a German working-class group, which later became international. It was at its congress in London in November, 1847, that Marx and Engels were entrusted with this task, and the League was dissolved in 1852, after its Central Board had been tried and imprisoned in the savage police reprisals that followed the defeat of the 1848 revolutions on the Continent. Thus the *Manifesto* soon became a manifesto without a party, but essentially it was and remained the practical program of a political party. Hence it was only right and proper that the position of the Communists vis-à-vis other socialist and radical groups should be defined. "The Communists do not form a separate party opposed to other working-class parties. They have no interests separate and apart from those of the proletariat as a whole." Thus communist victory is proletarian victory, and proletarian victory is to be the outcome of an inevitable historical process when the bourgeoisie has finally overreached itself.

But here a difficult problem is created. The course which Marx outlines as the course of history is one that he and Engels had in the main drawn from a study of the economic history of England and the political history of France. What is to happen where the bourgeoisie has not yet reached the point of digging its own graves, where the inhumanities of capitalism are still progressive, still necessary to the course of history? Marx believed, and continued to believe, what he was later to write in a preface to the *Critique of Political Economy*: that "no social form perishes until all the productive forces for which it provides scope have been developed." The *Manifesto* provides a political program, but it cannot be applied until the bourgeoisie begins its final self-destruction. What is to be done in the interim?

VI.

MARX'S
MATURE THEORY

THE QUESTION POSED at the end of the last chapter is not only practical, it is also theoretical. For it is not merely the question how the potential revolutionary is to behave in the interim between the present dilemmas of capitalism and its final catastrophes, but also how precisely one is to extrapolate from the theoretical analysis of the capitalist present a set of predictions about the character of the end of capitalism and the transition to socialism. In the earlier part of this book I traced the transformation of a theological view of human nature into the Hegelian philosophy of history, and the passage from the Hegelian themes of alienation and objectification to the language of would-be social science. In taking up the problems with which I shall be occupied in the latter part of this book, I shall inevitably-be concerned with questions regarding these two transitions: just how much theology survived in the Hegelian schematism, perhaps latently rather than manifestly, and how much of the Hegelian schematism survived into mature Marxism? These two questions must be answered before we can indicate the character of Marx's mature theory and the kind of authority which Marx's predictions therefore possess.

Some orthodox Communist writers as well as some, so to speak, orthodox anti-Communist writers have insisted that the writings of the young Marx on the topic of alienation represent at best a phase which Marx passed through and transcended, and that the mature theory can be understood in complete independence of these writings. Professor Lewis Feuer, for example, asserted in his "What is Alienation?—The Career of a Concept" (*New Politics*, 1962) that whereas the later Marx was clearly concerned with the centrality of the processes of productive work, the younger Marx used the concept of alienation in an entirely non-economic sense. Moreover, he asserts that the later Marx had abandoned both the concept and the expression. "The word 'alienation' was absent from Marx's mature analysis." Feuer's position might perhaps seem to gain support from that passage in the *Manifesto* in which Marx attacks the idealism of the Young Hegelians, whereby the abstract notion of the alienation of humanity had replaced the concrete struggles of living men. But once we have noted that this passage is susceptible of two interpretations, that it can be read either as a condemnation of any use of the concept of alienation (as Feuer's thesis would require) or as a condemnation of its abuse and misuse, we must go on and ask if there is any other evidence to support Feuer's position. There seems to be none. He is plainly wrong on the elementary question of the use of the word. In 1857-58, in the *Grundrisse*, Marx wrote about the development of human powers which characterizes modern society that "in bourgeois political economy—and in the epoch to which it corresponds—this complete elaboration of what lies within men appears as total alienation. . . ." Moreover, even when the word is absent, the concept is often present, for example, in the famous section in Volume I of *Capital* on the fetishism of commodities, and in the conception of freedom utilized in the later writings of Volume III. Furthermore, the use of the concept of alienation to expound economic matters is not, as we have already seen, new to the mature Marx. In the 1844 writings Marx had defined alienation in relation to work, money, economic relationships, and social class. If, then, writers such as Feuer are mistaken in denying the continuity of the notion of alienation in Marx's thought, what is its function in his mature thought?

Before answering this question it is necessary to distinguish between a schematism in accordance with which theories may be elaborated, and a substantive explanatory theory. By the latter I mean a theory by means of which a specified range of phenomena may be explained, in the sense that a model can be set out from the statement of which—together with other premises—the character of the phenomena in question can be deduced, and predictions of occurrences, other than those which the model was originally introduced to explain, can be derived. By the former I mean the type of model available for such use which may or may not find application in actual theories. By a model I mean the specification of an intelligible process (often of a simple mechanism) by means of which the observable features of a situation can be not merely correlated with one another, and not merely seen to stand in a causal relationship to one another, but seen to stand in such a relationship by virtue of the operation of the process specified in the model. So in the kinetic theory of gases the observable relationships between the pressure, temperature and volume of gases are explained by supposing gases to be composed of tiny, hard, impenetrable particles whose movements obey the laws of Newtonian mechanics. When, as with this particular theory, we can by means of the model not only connect the explanation of the behavior of gases with that of many other types of phenomena, but also specify a range of entities—atoms and molecules—about which further inquiries can be made and truths established, we are in a position to say that gases behave not only *as if* they were composed of particles but *because* they are composed of particles. Nonetheless, even an *as if* theory can be an important aid in organizing our knowledge of phenomena. And as with natural phenomena, so also with social phenomena.

The Hegelian concept of alienation may be understood as part of a model, available for application to different societies in different ways. To understand it like this would of course be to interpret it in a way that Hegel did not, but not necessarily in a way he would have objected to. For Hegel every set of social forms, or at least every pre-Hegelian set of social forms, is such that those who live in and through them are only partially conscious of the character of their society. Their alienation from themselves consists in the fact that they unknowingly maintain in being, by their activity, structures which at once frustrate the very possibilities which that same activity characteristically opens up. But in pushing to the limit these possibilities and so encountering the barriers of self-frustration, agents in a given society discover incoherences in their way of life which demand resolution. The attempt to resolve them is what dissolves one social order and brings about the institution of another. I have intentionally set all this out at a very general level, in order to make it clear that this is intended as a schematism applicable to any society—other than relatively simple ones—and which therefore must not depend for its form upon the particular features of certain societies.

This Hegelian model for understanding societies as necessarily self-destructive contrasts interestingly with alternative and rival models for such understanding. One example would be the type of conceptual scheme for sociological theory elaborated by Talcott Parsons, according to which a social system is to be viewed as a necessarily self-maintaining system in which imbalance at one point will call into being forces to restore equilibrium. The Parsonian model is not itself a theory explaining the phenomena of a particular society any more than the Hegelian model is. Parsons himself doubtless intends—just as Hegel did—that his schematism shall apply to all social phenomena. But it is at once clear that if rival and incompatible alternative conceptual schemes, such as the Hegelian and the Parsonian, are possible, then the contention that one of them must by some necessity apply to all possible societies becomes completely implausible. One might have thought that nobody would have been taken in by the *a priori* claims of a Hegelian *Logic*. But the attractiveness of this type of claim is made evident by its reappearance in a Parsonian guise. Whether in fact the phenomena of a given society are susceptible to analysis in Parsonian or in Hegelian terms, or indeed in neither, is an empirical question.

We have reached the point where we need to pass from the choice of models to the framing of substantive explanatory theory. The importance of these conceptual points for our present question is that Marx in his mature work is clearly advancing both a particular theory about the character of capitalism as a self-destructive form of social order, and a general philosophy of history according to which all forms of social order are in the end likely to be self-destructive and at the same time creative of new social orders. It is unclear whether Marx recognized that the kind of justification appropriate to explaining the phenomena of a particular social order is necessarily different from the kind of justification appropriate to a general philosophy of history. The former is a matter of science; the latter of what? Perhaps the characterization of the kind of justification appropriate to Marx's general philosophy of history will be easier if we examine how far ordinary scientific procedures will take Marx in the analysis of capitalism.

Marx's analysis of capitalism as a self-destructive system rests upon the thesis that capitalism must expand or perish and that it is bound to become less and less able to provide the resources necessary for its own expansion. Marx contends that in an unplanned, competitive market economy, the unhindered pursuit of profit by the individual entrepreneur is going to result in conflicts such as the continuous one between the requirement that labor costs be kept as low as possible (resulting in the restriction of demand) and the requirement that commodities be sold at prices that not only cover labor costs and cost of raw materials, but also provide profits (which necessitates effective demand for commodities beyond what is made available in purchasing power). The outcome of these conflicts will be that in the long run the entrepreneur will be confronted with a falling rate of profit and the worker with the impossibility of raising his standard of living beyond that required for the reproduction of the labor force. Two key predictions are derived from this analysis: the chronic impossibility of capitalism to distribute what it produces will result in crises in which investment will be drastically reduced, with the consequence of large fluctuations in unemployment; and the growth of large-scale industry will produce an organized and self-conscious working class which realizes that it has no interest in the continuance of this form of social and economic system.

For Marx's theory to be a successful attempt at scientific explanation a number of conditions have to be satisfied. For example, even if Marx's predictions had all turned out to be correct, Marxists would have had to show that the same predictions could not have been derived from any rival analysis. But I want to attend to a feature of Marx's analysis which attracts attention by the very way in which Marx's predictions have not been confirmed. Marx treats capitalism as an economic system in which not only are entrepreneur and proletarian assigned roles that, in place of their individual wills, determine how they behave, but these roles are represented as being fixed and unalterable. Marx emphasizes this in the Preface to *Capital*, in exempting the individual capitalist from blame for the workings of the capitalist system. The entrepreneur cannot modify his behavior in order to annul or at least modify the self-destructive aspects of that behavior. But why not? Is it that the individual capitalist cannot hope to become conscious of the truths asserted in *Capital*? Or is it that even if he does become conscious of them—even if the capitalist class collectively becomes conscious of them—he cannot, for some other reason, alter his behavior? What Marx would have answered to these questions is not entirely clear. What is clear is that Marx's analysis of capitalism is a correct analysis of its workings only so long as the capitalist does not become conscious of those workings in a way that enables him to modify them. Seen in this light, Marx's analysis is no more impugned by the incorrectness of his predictions than would a description of the working of a heat engine, which predicted a certain outcome on the assumption that there would be no intervention from outside to interfere with the working of the system described. But if this is a correct answer to the conventional accusation that Marx's work is not scientific, it makes it all the more plain that insofar as Marx's theory of the workings of capitalism is part of science, his predictions are bound to be conditional. Yet at more than one point Marx appears to predict *unconditionally* not merely the intensifying crisis of capitalism but the transition to socialism. Why does he feel able to do this? Again Marx himself gives no clear answer. Both in the *Manifesto* and in *Capital* there is an astonishing lacuna whenever the question of the nature of the transition to socialism is raised, a point at which rhetoric takes over from theory. In the *Manifesto* Marx had described the outcome of class struggle as being either the victory of one class over the other or "the ruin of the contending classes." Elsewhere—in a letter to the editorial board of a Russian journal, for example—he clearly allows for alternative outcomes of historical sequences. Why then in this case does he apparently envisage no possible future outcome to the class struggle within capitalism but its suppression by first socialism and then the classless society of communism?

Let me make this point in another way. Karl Popper has, in *The Poverty of Historicism*, accused Marx of failing to distinguish between a law and a trend. A law is a statement of a regularity such that of two classes of event the occurrence of an event of the one kind is a sufficient (and perhaps also a necessary) condition for the occurrence of an event of the other kind. A knowledge of the laws which hold in a given situation is never by itself sufficient to enable us to predict. To predict we must know both the relevant laws—which enable us to infer correctly from the occurrence of certain causes the occurrence of certain effects—and, in addition, the antecedent and concomitant conditions which hold. A man who tries to make predictions without a knowledge of these is a man who tries to infer the conclusion that "an event of type Y will occur" from the premise "whenever an event of type X occurs, an event of type Y will occur," without seeing that he can only derive his conclusion validly if he is also able to assert that "an event of type X will occur"—or some other such minor premise—and to do this he must be certain that no external interests will prevent the occurrence of an event of type X.

A trend is a sequence of historical events moving in a certain uniform direction. Clearly one cannot predict a trend without knowledge of both the relevant laws and the relevant antecedent and concomitant conditions; but when Popper accuses Marx of trying to predict trends unconditionally, that is, independently of antecedent and accompanying circumstance, he is making a mistake. For Marx in the letter mentioned above makes precisely the distinction to which Popper says that he is blind. Precisely on the basis of this distinction, he refuses to predict that Russian society will inevitably pass through the same historical stages passed through by Western Europe. Yet to some extent Popper's contention is correct; for if Marx is prepared in this context to allow for the possibility of alternative types of development, why is he so sure in others that the end product of such development will be socialism? Why in this one case does he see history as having only one goal? Is it because he is involved in the confusion of which Popper accuses him?

To raise the same point in a sharper way: the young Marx in the 1844 writings had diagnosed the belief of bourgeois economists and others that the laws governing economic behavior in a capitalist economy were eternal and inviolable ordinances which made certain types of happening inevitable as a symptom of the false consciousness engendered by the alienation characteristic of their society. But this belief in inevitability, or something very like it, now seems to appear in Marx's own thought as part of his belief about the transition to socialism. Is this really the case? What I want to suggest in reply commits me to an interpretation of Marx's thought which is in many ways at odds with Engels' interpretation of that thought. To dismiss Engels as having misunderstood Marx is by now an altogether familiar move; Lukacs did it long ago. But just for that reason one is all too apt to suppose that this dismissal does not itself involve difficulties. For if it is a mistake to treat Engels as an authentic interpreter of Marx, the first person to make that mistake was Marx himself. And yet the whole form of Engels' presentation of Marxism is so different from Marx's that it is difficult to see the same doctrine in the two writers.

Engels presents Marxism as a systematic philosophy of nature as well as of society, according to which certain highest-order laws govern all natural and social processes, and the evolutionary order of nature is matched by that of social progress. Engels had indeed put behind him the Hegelian Marxism of the early writings by the time he propounded the total metaphysical system contained in *Anti-Dühring*. For him the transition to socialism is scientifically predictable on the basis of a knowledge of the relevant laws. Engels' comparison of Marx with Darwin, which was cited in the last chapter, is characteristic of Engels' assimilation of social science to natural science. Engels is not necessarily mistaken in principle about this assimilation; but of course if Engels' interpretation of Marx is correct, then Marxism is indeed vulnerable to criticism such as Popper's. It is therefore important to point out that Marxism is susceptible of another interpretation, one which relies upon the continuity of Marx's thought and upon the survival of the concept of alienation in his mature writings, and so returns us to the question that I posed at the outset of this chapter. Although we ought to be reluctant to differ from Engels about the interpretation of Marx, we may have to overcome this reluctance.

As I construed the Hegelian concept of alienation, it is meant to pick out those features of the structures of social systems which simultaneously release certain human energies and make the accomplishment of certain goals possible, but also frustrate other possibilities and inhibit other energies. The actors involved in these patterns of behavior do not recognize the source of this frustration as residing in the forms of their own activity; in this consists their alienation from themselves. The new society, which is founded upon the resolution of the incongruities and the destruction of the frustrations of the old, always allows expression to hitherto inhibited possibilities, and in this sense the newer society is an advance upon the old. In other words, the Hegelian concept rests upon a hope, is founded on a confidence in what human beings will be able to make of their lives when certain barriers and frustrations are removed. This humanism Hegel, and after him Marx, inherit from the eighteenth century. The hope that constitutes this humanism has to be carefully distinguished both from the religious faith that was its predecessor, and from the scientistic dependence on would-be predictions of inevitable progress into which it has often degenerated.

It is possible to construe this hope as partially justified by the past history of human achievement. But Marxist humanism is in no sense based upon the kind of empirical generalization that could warrant—in anything like the way in which scientific predictions are warranted—so specific a prediction as that of the transition to socialism. More light is thrown upon this point when we consider the content of this prediction. When Marx wrote that men never formulate a problem until they have the resources to solve it, he envisaged the history of society as analogous to the history of science, and his confidence in the non-existence of insoluble problems resembled that of the scientist. But just as the scientist cannot say in advance of providing an authentic solution to his problem what that solution will be—although he may be able to specify certain characteristics that any solution must possess—so in Marx's view we cannot say in advance what content the solution to the problems of contemporary society will have, although we can specify certain necessary characteristics. Hence there is very little in Marx's writings about the nature of socialism or communism. For socialism and communism will be solutions to the problems posed in a form of society in which the price men pay for learning to control and exploit nature—the great and characteristic achievement of bourgeois society—is controlled and exploited by the very social forms they brought about in the course of their encounter with nature. Socialism is specified minimally as a stage of society in which men are rewarded according to their contribution, communism as one in which they are rewarded according to their needs. In both, private ownership of the means of production and the unplanned anarchy of the pursuit of profit are replaced by communally owned and directed production for need and for enjoyment; but a few other bare and sparse remarks do no more than indicate what the transition from the realm of necessity to that of freedom, what the overcoming of alienation will consist of. And it is of the essence of the Marxist case that this absence of elaboration or specificity should be so. For socialism, precisely because it is the overcoming of alienation, must be a self-consciously constructed society in which institutions transparently serve the human purposes of those who construct them. This is why the emancipation of the working class can only be the task of the working class itself; it cannot be accomplished for and on behalf of them by anyone else. Equally, this is why the form of the society they will construct in the course of emancipating themselves cannot be prescribed to them by anyone else in advance of their own decisions, and hence cannot be predicted.

Marx's confidence that capitalism would be replaced by socialism and not by some new form of class society turns out to rest upon foundations quite different from his confidence that capitalism would in the long run exhibit certain characteristics derived from the maintenance of a chronic tendency to underconsumption, combined with the growth of large-scale industrial enterprises and working-class organization. The latter is a matter of social science; the former a matter of a humanistic belief in the possibilities and resources of human nature. This belief, without which Marxism as a political movement would be unintelligible, is a secularized version of a Christian virtue. But just as Christianity has been much better at describing the state of fallen men than the glories of redeemed men, so Marxism is better at explaining what alienation consists of than in describing the future nature of unalienated men. Yet it is clear that the concept of a human nature freed from alienation is not an empty one, and that its content cannot be understood apart from its origins. Man rescued from alienation will be liberated man, but in what will his liberty consist? It will be a liberty to create his life in a way analogous to that in which an artist creates. "Man also creates according to the laws of beauty," Marx wrote in 1844, and in Marx's vocabulary there are many reminiscences of the terms in which Schiller had described the artist as an ideal of the Romantic movement. The productive work which constitutes man's central activity in the world is at present something that constrains and inhibits most of our creativity; the ending of alienation will transform work into a creative activity to be judged by aesthetic standards.

I began this chapter by posing two questions: first, how does Marx extrapolate from the dilemmas of capitalism its future overthrow and replacement? Second, does the concept of alienation survive into his mature writings? I have answered that we cannot reply correctly to the former unless we reply correctly to the latter. Engels, who turns his back upon the concept of alienation—and, indeed, upon the whole Hegelian inheritance of Marxism—cannot, in his interpretation, do justice to the extent to which Marx insists that there is more to any social situation than what is empirically given; the possibilities in a human situation always transcend what can be observed. Instead, Engels falls back upon a false scien-

tific metaphysics and we get the mechanistic and deterministic formulas introducēd into Marxism which
for fifty years defined its style of thought. But the introduction of these formulas was not simply an intellectual mistake on Engels' part. It was a response to
a dilemma posed by the very structure of Marx's
thought.

Marx altered his view of the agencies by which
the organization and actual execution of the transition
to socialism would be carried out. In 1848 he obviously had an insurrectionary model of future events
in mind, derived from his study of the first French
Revolution. Later on, the parties of the Labor Movement became centrally important, and the example of
the Paris Commune of 1871 moved him profoundly.
But he was in fact uncommitted to any of the organizational alternatives. There are in his writings scat-
tered remarks about the appropriate character of political organization for Marxist revolutionaries on
which both Leninists and their opponents were able
to draw in later struggles. But Marx's own pragmatism
on this point was limited only by his anxiety to ex-
clude certain alternatives that would either have deprived the working class of any authentic political
voice of its own by a process of collusion and com-
promise with the ruling forces of society, or reduced

the political organizations of the working class to an unrepresentative sectarianism. Lassalle and some English trade unionists represented the former alternative, Bakunin the latter. Marx's own organizational commitments indicate no more of a detailed prescription of how the revolutionary is to bridge the gap between the present and the future than does his theory of the transition.

The critical character of the problem, which Marx in consequence bequeathed to his political heirs, is underlined by considering the rival, incompatible, and always defective solutions that different groups among them produced. There are first of all those who follow Engels in treating Marx's view of the future as a set of super-predictions based on the analysis of the process of history: we must await the coming of the revolution as we await the coming of an eclipse. Just as for the moment, while the planets move through their predetermined positions, all we can do is grind lenses, mount telescopes, and wait; so while capitalism moves through its predetermined course of development we must prepare ourselves by organizing and engaging in trade-union activity. There is a strain of this kind in a great deal of later Marxism: Dimitrov compared history to a turning wheel and Trotsky compared it to the ebb and flow of tides. In German social democracy and Russian Menshevism this trend came to dominate all others. In the theories of Kautsky the gap between the reformist present and the revolutionary future becomes widened to the point at which Kautsky, from his own resources, would have found it very hard to counter the more clearheaded and self-conscious reformism of Bernstein. Bernstein's theory indeed articulated Kautsky's practice far more authentically than Kautsky's own self-avowed revolutionary position. Happily for himself, in the struggle against Bernstein, Kautsky was able to make use of Rosa Luxemburg's genuine revolutionary position and passion. But even if Rosa Luxemburg is far closer to the moral substance of Marx's own position, even she found no bridge between predictions about the economic development of capitalism and beliefs about a socialist future, except for a faith in the direction in which the spontaneity of the working masses would move them.

Kautsky was forced to answer Bernstein's reformism on Bernstein's own chosen ground. Marx had predicted the decline of capitalism; Bernstein pointed to the fact of its steady expansion. Marx had predicted the radicalization of the working class; Bernstein pointed to the fact of its growing domestication. Kautsky, to answer Bernstein, had therefore either to deny that the facts were as Bernstein claimed, or to introduce subsidiary hypotheses to explain why the facts were not incompatible with Marx's explanations.

In the face of Bernstein's position, however, it is possible to offer a quite different kind of response, the kind of response offered by Lukacs in 1922 in *History and Class Consciousness*. Lukacs had a profound sensitivity to the presence of the themes of alienation and reification in Marx's mature writings, which allowed him to formulate as Marx's central positions propositions which Marx only formulated fully and explicitly in the 1844 manuscripts, the existence of which was unknown at the time of Lukacs' writing. On the basis of these formulations Lukacs tried to rescue Marxism from falsification by reason of predictive error, by claiming that the truth of Marx's analyses was independent of their predictive power. This alone would have involved him in a quarrel with such interpreters of Marxism as Engels, Plekhanov, and Bukharin. But Lukacs insists that since Marxism reveals that men who have hitherto been dominated by processes and forces which they could not recognize or understand are now at the point in history at which they are able in a fully self-conscious way to liberate themselves from these processes and forces, Marxism entails the marking of a sharp contrast between the law-governed past and the open future.

Just as Hegel had contended that we can only understand the patterns of historical development after they have occurred, so Lukacs argues that the Marxist interpretation of previous social orders and of capitalism as law-governed in their developments is essentially an after-the-event interpretation. Marxism reveals the reified nature of life in the past, and it is able to reveal this because Marxism is the articulation of a consciousness no longer mystified by such reification. The future of which Marxism speaks is not a future determined by laws and predicted by passive spectators of the law-governed processes of history; it is a future that will be constructed in accordance with the intentions of those same self-conscious agents whose consciousness is articulated by Marxist theory. For Lukacs, Marxism is not just a theoretical analysis advanced by an individual theorist—an analysis that is true or false in terms of its correspondence to an external social reality, the truth or falsity of which can be shown only by the power of the theory to generate predictions about such a reality. Rather, Marxism is that consciousness which is constitutive of contemporary social reality—contemporary, that is, for the age to which both Marx and Lukacs belong—and as such is itself a basic social datum.

Who are the selves of whom Marxism is the self-consciousness? Lukacs answers that they are the proletarians, the class continuously created and recreated by the capitalist system, but which can find no satisfaction for its wants and needs within the capitalist system. Does this mean that any and every proletarian must be a Marxist? Lukacs relies on Marx's assertion that it is not a question of the attitudes of this or that particular proletarian, but of the attitudes of the proletarian as such, or—to use a terminology other than Marx's—of the role assigned to the proletarian by the system. But if the actual, empirical proletarians do not in fact exhibit that self-consciousness articulated by Marxism, what then?

Lukacs replies that true proletarian consciousness is embodied in the Communist Party, that group of proletarians which defines its own existence in Marxist terms, and by so doing has become the agent of history. Is this claim of Lukacs only what most critics have seen it as being, an arbitrary and indefensible act of faith in the Communist Party? Such critics have, I think, failed to separate two quite distinct positions taken by Lukacs. On the one hand, Lukacs conceived of the Communist Party as an organization dedicated to preserving the openness of history and continually summoning the proletarians to shape their own future. On the other hand, he identified this ideal Communist Party of his theorizing with the parties of the Third International as they actually existed. But in so doing he committed himself to the acceptance of those parties as the only legitimate interpreters of the history of his own age. This in practice meant accepting the leaderships of those parties, and the response of those leaderships was at once to denounce Lukacs. So the logic of his own theorizing committed Lukacs to denouncing himself. Which he did. The theorists of the Third International condemned what they saw as Lukacs' subjectivism, voluntarism, and revolutionary romanticism. The road to socialism is law-governed because all history is law-governed and moves forward inevitably—this became the central doctrine of Stalinism in which all the deterministic and mechanistic elements in Engels' thought were accentuated. History, according to Stalin, moves forward whether we will it or not; we can assist it or try to retard it, but we cannot change its direction or its goal. By his self-abnegation, first in the face of Zinoviev and the leaders of the Third International, and then in the face of Stalinism, Lukacs at least paid lip-service to key doctrines identical with those of the Kautskyism he had fought. Kautsky was condemned by name under Stalin, but Stalinism borrowed more from Kautsky than from Lenin.

Kautsky or Lukacs? The dilemma which the choice between them constitutes is the dilemma of how we are to extrapolate, from our understanding of the past and the present, our beliefs about the future —a dilemma which, so I have been arguing, lies at the very heart of Marxism. The failure to solve it leads Marxists to oscillate between a Kautskyist confidence in the objective march of history and a Lukacsian confidence in themselves. In both cases it is difficult for them not to regress into the theological modes of thought in which their problem had its origin. A deification of the Party, or a deification of history, or both, was the fate that awaited them. The criteria of deification are clear. A man or a group have been deified when their pronouncements are treated as authoritative and unfalsifiable, whatever the independent evidence about the subject matter on which they pronounce. That is to say, when the evidence and the pronouncements conflict, if it is established that it is the evidence that must be explained away, then deification has occurred. It need not, of course, be deification of the person or group concerned; for they may claim to speak only in the name of some other transcendent ideal. In this case, it is the alleged ideal being who is deified. On these criteria Stalinism clearly deified both Stalin and history, while other variants of Marxism have tended toward deification of a similar kind. I have already called such deification a regressive tendency. Marx pointed out Feuerbach's failure to demystify Hegel completely, and Hegel's failure to demystify Christianity. He traced both failures to their inability to transcend the social order to which they belonged. Stalinism required a similar unmasking: Stalin remystified and reinstated the metaphysical fictions from which, step by step, Hegel, Feuerbach, and Marx had freed themselves. Marx would have diagnosed the roots of Stalinism as being in the social order of the class society in the Soviet Union which Stalin had helped to create, that of bureaucratic state capitalism.

We thus find the paradox of Marxists simultaneously repeating the positions of Feuerbach and Marx against religion, while recreating in their own practice the very same religious phenomena with which Feuerbach and Marx were concerned as critics. The full impact of that paradox will not be felt until we have considered in more detail Marx's view of religion.

VII.

MARXISM AND RELIGION

ACCORDING TO MARX, religion has a dual role to play. Throughout the history of class society religion performs two essential functions: it buttresses the established order by sanctifying it and by suggesting that the political order is somehow ordained by divine authority, and it consoles the oppressed exploited by offering them in heaven what they are denied upon earth. At the same time, by holding before them a vision of what they are denied, religion plays at least partly a progressive role in that it gives the common people some idea of what a better order would be. But when it becomes possible to realize that better order upon earth in the form of communism, then religion becomes wholly reactionary, for it distracts men from establishing a now possible good society on earth by still turning their eyes toward heaven. Its sanctification of the existing social order makes it a counter-revolutionary force. Thus in the course of building a communist society, the Marxist must fight religion because it will inevitably stand in his path. But in a communist society there will be no need to persecute religion, for its essential functions will have disappeared. There will no longer be an exploiting class, nor will the common people stand in need of religious consolations. Religion itself will disappear of its own accord without persecution. (This is an interesting example of the functionalism embodied in Marxism; the state, too, according to Marx and Lenin, will wither away when it becomes functionless.)

In origin, nevertheless, religion may be genuinely revolutionary, a real attempt to abolish exploitation. It only becomes other-wordly when its attempts to transform this world fail. Then its hope of the good society is transferred to another world, and in ideal form compensates for man's powerlessness to realize his ideal. Engels saw Christianity as having undergone this change. "The history of early Christianity has many characteristic points of contact with the present labor movement. Like the latter, Christianity was at first a movement of the oppressed; it began as a reli-

gion of the slaves and the freed, the poor and out-
lawed, of the peoples defeated and crushed by the
force of Rome. Both Christianity and Proletarian Socialism preached the coming deliverance from slavery
and poverty. . . ." (*On the History of Early Christianity*, I.) Engels goes on to say that whereas socialism puts this deliverance on earth, Christianity puts it
in heaven. Kautsky, however, in *The Foundations
of Christianity*, was prepared to go further. "The liberation from poverty which Christianity declared was
at first thought of quite realistically. It was to take
place in the world and not in Heaven." The trans-
ference of liberation to heaven only took place later.

Thus the essential mark of latter-day religion is
its other-worldliness. It places far off the salvation
that socialism brings near. It has its origin in man's
sense of his powerlessness in this world. Engels
continually emphasizes man's feeling of powerlessness
before nature in speaking of the origins of primitive
religion. But it is not only before nature that man is
powerless; he is also overwhelmed by society, so that
the processes of society appear to man as strange and
terrible divinities. Thus in ancient Greek religion the
power of necessity, *ananke*, was personified. The
Marxist scholar George Thomson writes in *Aeschy-
lus and Athens* that "throughout Greek literature, from

Homer onwards, the ideas of *ananke*, 'necessity,' and *douleia*, 'slavery,' are intimately connected, the former being habitually employed to denote both the state of slavery as such and the hard labors and tortures to which slaves are subjected. . . . During the maturity of the city-state the idea of *ananke* was developed and extended. Not only was the slave under the absolute control of his master and denied all share in the surplus product of his labor, but the master himself, in the conditions of a monetary economy, was at the mercy of forces which he was unable to control; and so the freeman, too, was enslaved to the blind force of necessity, which frustrated his desires and defeated his efforts. But if necessity is supreme, and her action incalculable, all change appears subjectively as chance; and so by the side of *ananke* there arose the figure of *tyche*—opposite poles of the same conception. The belief that the world is ruled by *tyche* can be traced through Euripides to Pindar, who declared that she was one of the *moirai* and the strongest of them all; and during the next two centuries, the cult of *tyche* became one of the most widespread and popular in Greece." This passage is characteristic of the Marxist contention that the gods are personifications of the powers that dominate human life. When such powers no longer dominate man, there will no longer be gods.

This is how Marxism hopes to abolish religion. But there remains the initial assumption—that religion needs to be accounted for. Marxism seems to assume from the outset that religion is palpably false. How is it able to do so?

The answer to this lies in Marx's materialism. Since matter is the primary reality, the possibility of the existence of a god or of gods is excluded. This leads to two questions: What is involved in Marx's materialism? And in what sort of a god is belief excluded by materialism? Marx inherited his materialism from Feuerbach; but all Feuerbach had said was that being precedes consciousness, not consciousness being. This assertion is one that could be made by many religious believers. The question is always one of the nature of being, not of its priority. By "being" Marx and Feuerbach both mean "all that is" and the assertion of the primacy of being becomes materialism only because of the additional belief that everything that is, is a more or less complicated organization of atoms. Engels uses the formula "matter in motion" to cover this. Since everything is explicable ultimately in terms of matter in motion, religious explanations of any event are excluded. This at once brings us to the answer to our second question. Religion is conceived by the Marxist as offering explanations of phenomena which are alternatives to scientific explanation. Science explains in terms of a this-worldly causation, religion in terms of an other-worldly causation. Thus religion is only disposed of by the Marxist critique if it is true that the essential character of religion is other-worldliness, its essential claim to explain phenomena, and its essential function to compensate for human powerlessness and to mask human exploitation. This thesis we must now examine.

It must be granted that the Marxist critique holds true for a great deal of religion, and in particular for a great deal of nineteenth-century religion. The doctrine of the Tractarians, for example, helps to illustrate the critique. Suspiciously enough, the doctrines of priesthood and of apostolic succession were rediscovered by Anglicans just at the time when the state was beginning to deny in its practice any real difference between nonconformity and the Church of England. High churchmanship replaced social eminence as the mark of the staunch Anglican. The ascetic disciplines which the Tractarians commended were of a kind possible only to a leisured class; their sacramental doctrines were irrelevant in an industrial society. F. D. Maurice wrote of their view of baptism in 1838: "Where is the minister of Christ in London, Birmingham or Manchester, whom such a doctrine, heartily and inwardly entertained, would not drive to madness? He is sent to preach the Gospel. What Gospel? Of all the thousands whom he addresses, he cannot venture to believe that there are ten who, in Dr. Pusey's sense, retain their baptismal purity. All he can do, therefore, is to tell wretched creatures, who spend eighteen hours out of the twenty-four in close factories and bitter toil, corrupting and being corrupted, that if they spend the remaining six in prayer—he need not add fasting—they may possibly be saved. How can we insult God and torment man with such mockery?" There was another side to the doctrine of the Tractarians; but of a great deal of what they and churchmen of every persuasion taught the Marxist critique was and remains true.

Yet if it is this side of the Marxist critique that has dominated Marxist attitudes to religion in practice at most times and places, there has also persisted within Marxism a quite different emphasis upon religion as not merely "the opiate of the people" and "the sigh of the oppressed creature," but also "the heart of a heartless world." (Contribution to The Critique of Hegel's Philosophy of Right.) Nor is this surprising when one recalls yet another aspect of the predictive failures of Marxism. Marx viewed religion as having in the present and future—as contrasted to the past—a wholly reactionary role, because he assumed that a completely secular world view could not but be adopted by the working class, let alone by progressive intellectuals. Both Marx and Engels took it for granted that the intellectual case against religion had been made by the materialists and the skeptics of the eighteenth century. Insofar as their arguments still failed to convince, it was because religion was not a matter of the intellect, but of social needs. If the social factors which produced these needs were removed by transforming the structure of society, then religion would become functionless and would wither away. Indeed, Marx and Engels believed this to be already happening. They regarded the English as peculiarly backward, but Engels, who chided the English for their insular attachment to religion, believed that by the 1850's continental influences of a skeptical and atheistic kind were moving even the respectable middle classes. Skepticism, as he put it, had come in with salad oil. The English working class Engels regarded as much further along the road toward complete secularization. Already in 1844 he had envisaged the victory of unbelief as all but accomplished. Yet in two important respects he was mistaken.

The first and less important concerns the actual history of secularization; it has been slower and less effective in England than Engels predicted. The Catholic Church, for example, in England as elsewhere, has retained the allegiance of some sections of the industrial working class. But more important is a second and quite different type of error. For secularization has not resulted, as I noted in the opening paragraphs of this book, in the working classes—or indeed any other social group as a group—acquiring a new and more rational set of beliefs about the nature of man and the world. Rather, men have been deprived of any over-all view and to this extent have been deprived of one possible source of understanding and of action. Thus, at least so far as advanced industrial societies are concerned, outside those societies where Marxism is propagated by the state, the conditions which are inimical to religion seem to be inimical to Marxism too. Apparent exceptions to this seem indeed to be only apparent. The nominal Marxist allegiance of a large section of the French working class, for example, is only the attenuated content of the old radical secularism in a new dress; and as French society develops technologically and technocratically, it too is eroded.

In such a situation the adherents and sympathizers of Marxism have not unnaturally been more apt to note resemblances between Marxism and Christianity of just the kind with which I have been concerned.

Insensitivity to them has on the whole been exhibited only by the hostile critics of Marxism. Marx and Engels long ago proclaimed Thomas Münzer as a spiritual ancestor; and modern Marxists have written several sympathetic studies of millenarian religion. How odd, then, that the resemblances between revolutionary Marxism and such religions have been noted by some critics as a necessarily discrediting fact. The unsatisfactory character of such discussions is in part due to the unexamined liberal, secular assumptions of the critics. It is also, however, due in part to a failure to distinguish different features of the analogy between Marxism and Christianity.

Both Marxism and Christianity rescue individual lives from the insignificance of finitude (to use an Hegelian expression) by showing the individual that he has or can have some role in a world-historical drama. The dramatic metaphor is not unimportant here. Marx, in the *Eighteenth Brumaire of Louis Bonaparte*, saw the function of ideology in past revolutions as providing a dramatic framework which events themselves would otherwise have lacked. But the revolution of the nineteenth century was, in his words, to "draw its poetry from the future." No dramaturge, but history itself, is now needed. Christianity cannot dispense with the notion of men having parts in a cosmic drama. The liturgy is the reenactment of this notion. But if religion is able to create an identity that transcends the identity which the existing social order confers upon individuals and within which it would like to confine them (so that it is the message of reactionary religion that it is God himself who wishes to confine us "in that station" to which he has been pleased to call us), it is also true that the sacrifice of individuals for eternal purposes is inherent in religion, and both sides of this phenomenon are carried over into Marxism.

The process by which they are carried over cannot be understood apart from that whole regression of Marxism which I discussed in the last chapter and which originated in the deification of the Party or of history or of both. This reemergence of ideal entities in the history of Marxism renders intelligible those surface phenomena of Marxism which are so obviously religious that it has become trite to remark upon them. The cultic preservation of Lenin's body is an outstanding example. Still obvious but of far greater significance is the treatment of deviations of belief. Clearly someone who has been a Marxist may alter his beliefs on some point in such a way that common action with his former comrades becomes impossible; but it has often been the case in Marxist movements that common assent is required to beliefs which do not involve immediate action or action in the foreseeable future, and as far as rival predictions are concerned, there has been little attempt by Marxists to agree on a way in which their differences might be settled and the outcome awaited. Creedal uniformity, as in religion, often seems to be valued by Marxists for its own sake. The disciplining of the Soviet economist Varga for his view of postwar Europe is the kind of case I have in mind. This example also underlines the fact that the failure of Marxism to free itself from its religious heritage has made it easier for Marxists to elaborate a concept of science quite other than that of Marx and Engels. Both of them had the kind of interest in the progress of science not uncharacteristic of their age. Engels' own writings on science are of extremely dubious value. But it is fair to say that he accepted natural science as a continuing activity with its own standards and methods. The notion that there could be a peculiarly Marxist science as opposed to "bourgeois science" is alien to his thought. The roots of this Stalinist notion lie in the religious concept of beliefs about the world not having to derive their validity from the observed facts. Lysenko's fraudulent experiments are the counterpart to those fraudulent cases of miraculous weeping or bleeding statues which the Bolsheviks at one time so delighted in exposing in their anti-God exhibitions.

But too much attention to these relatively surface phenomena may be misleading; they belong to the corruption of Marxism, and if Marxism is corruptible, this is, as Marxists themselves should have well understood, a possible fate of any doctrine that functions as the expression of social forces. Christians who make use of this kind of point in order to criticize Marxism as a whole ought to remember that it is precisely what Marxism has in common with Christianity that has rendered it so particularly vulnerable. Liberals who produce this kind of critique all too often wish to ignore the Marxist critique of liberalism. Both liberals and Christians are too apt to forget that Marxism is the only systematic doctrine in the modern world that has been able to translate to any important degree the hopes men once expressed, and could not but express in religious terms, into the secular project of understanding societies and expressions of human possibility and history as a means of liberating the present from the burdens of the past, and so constructing the future. Liberalism by contrast simply abandons the virtue of hope. For liberals the future has become the present enlarged. Christianity remains irremediably tied to a social content it ought to

disown. Marxism as historically embodied phenomenon may have been deformed in a large variety of
ways. But the Marxist project remains the only one
we have for reestablishing hope as a social virtue.

VIII.

THREE PERSPECTIVES ON MARXISM

MARXISM CAN BE viewed in at least three distinct ways by a member of a modern Western society: as substantially true and therefore to be adhered to; as substantially false and therefore to be contested and fought; or as a doctrine we cannot adhere to because there are truths which it cannot accommodate, yet also a doctrine we cannot entirely discard because it embodies truths inseparable from their connection with Marx's general theoretical formulations. This last point must necessarily remain obscure until it has been expounded at some length; but it is worth remarking even now that if it is correct it may at least in part explain both why some thinkers who are, or plainly ought to be, aware of the truths that Marxism cannot consistently acknowledge, choose to ignore these truths, and why some thinkers who have declared and to their own satisfaction demonstrated that Marxism is plainly false, yet feel the need to reiterate their demonstrations in circumstances which strongly suggest that it is not other people whom they are trying to convince. No modern doctrine has been refuted and continues to be refuted as often as Marxism has been and is, and explanations of this fact in terms of the psychopathology of the individuals concerned are as speculative and as unsound as such explanations usually are.

Those who wish to insist that Marxism is substantially true are faced with two major difficulties: the impotence of Marxist economic theory (as contrasted with the vast analytical skill of Marx's work as an economic historian and as a historian of economic theory) and the fate of Marx's predictions. The former they usually ignore; the latter they generally confront with one of two strategies, normally exclusive alternatives, but sometimes combined. The first of these orginated with Mehring; it consists in the assertion that Marx and Engels, although substantially right about the sequence of events to come, were wrong about the time scale. Until after 1945 this maneuver had perhaps *some* plausibility by itself. A deep inability to distribute for consumption what it produced, and a related inability to provide continuously the growing investment that it needed for its own expansion, continued to characterize the uneven patterns of capitalist growth. Even so, the counterpart in Marx's predictions to that of the growth of capitalistic crisis, namely, that of the growth of a *revolutionary* working class, had not occurred. And this, at least, had to be explained by supplementary hypotheses. The supplementary hypothesis which tended to dominate Marxist movements was that sections of the working class had been bought off by being granted a share in the prosperity of the owning classes and that in consequence the working class had been deprived of its natural revolutionary leadership. The prevalence of these hypotheses among Marxists—and the addition to them of the doctrine that doctrinal corruption, not only among reformist socialists, but also among self-avowed revolutionaries, had intensified the crisis of leadership—helped to blind Marxists to two key facts. The first of these was that the working class—and not just its leadership—was either reformist or unpolitical except in the most exceptional of situations, not so much because of the inadequacies of its trade union and political leadership as because of its whole habit of life. This habit of life was sustained and changed by a growth in the standard of living in the working class which depended in turn on the continued, if uneven, growth of capitalist economies. When, in the early 1930's, Trotsky was confronted with the facts of this growth by the Marxist economist Fritz Sternberg he remarked that he had had no time recently to study the statistics; that on the truth or falsity of the statements involved much else that he was committed to depended he does not seem to have noticed. Nor was this attitude restricted to Trotsky, whom I select here as the most honest, perceptive, and intelligent of post-1930 Marxists.

But if the need to elaborate Marx's analysis by the addition of supplementary hypotheses, which explained why the facts were not as his predictions had suggested they would be, was already strongly felt in the period from 1900 to 1945, it obviously became more acute in the postwar period in which the ability of capitalism to innovate in order to maintain its equilibrium and its expansion was of a radically new kind. State intervention, the planning of the market, the creation of new relations between the state and the large corporations, the management of the flow of credit were all born in the earlier period; but the political and social recognition of the need for self-conscious management of the economy as a whole rendered obsolete the notion of capitalism as essentially a form of unplanned economy to which state intervention was alien except in marginal cases. Consequently, not only has the future crisis of capitalism had—for those who wished to retain the substance of the classical Marxist view—to be delayed, there had to be additional explanations why, in the new situation, capitalism is still liable to crisis in the same sense as before.

The same facts of capitalist development are also an embarrassment to those who undertake a quite different maneuver in relation to Marx's predictions: Those who treat his boldest prediction of all, that concerning the transition to socialism, as having already come true in the Soviet Union and other countries of the East-European bloc. But the only criterion in terms of which these countries could be called socialist is that according to which a country is socialist if and only if the means of production are owned by the state. Such a criterion of socialism was plausible only when capitalism defined itself in terms of the notion of an unplanned market, and even then state ownership was never envisaged as more than a precondition of socialism. For if the state owns the means of production, the vital question becomes: who owns the state? Marx envisaged a socialist state as necessarily more democratic (in a very plain sense of "democratic") than any bourgeois state. By contrast these later would-be Marxists are forced to allow that a socialist economy can coexist with a political power that is monopolized by a small elite.

All these are familiar—even over-familiar— points. What is less familiar: those who adopt these points have characteristically become unable to offer any account of their reasons for adopting the moral and the political allegiance that they do. Why this is so will become plainer if we turn from considering the theoretical question of what has happened to Marx's predictions to the practical question of what being a Marxist does or could consist in, nowadays, in the Western world, and contrast it with what holding his theories meant for Marx. For Marx theory was to inform and direct the activities of a party and a class which had been brought into existence by social agencies which could be comprehended only by his theory. Theory was to give vision and articulate an explicit definition to political and moral stances forced upon individuals in consequence of the positions they occupy in the social system. Theory is precisely not a set of opinions which individuals may or may not happen to choose to adopt. But just this is what Marxism has become: a set of "views" which stand in no kind of organic relationship to an individual's social role or identity, let alone his real position in the class structure. And in becoming like this, Marxism has been "practiced" in precisely the same way as that in which religious beliefs have been practiced in modern secularized societies. Just as religion becomes a private talismanic aid for the individual, helping him to orient himself to the everyday world, so very often does Marxism. Hegel said that reading the newspaper had become for modern man the equivalent of and replacement for the practice of morning prayer. And for the modern radical intellectual holding Marxist views often stands to a certain kind of reading of the newspaper as holding certain theological views does to a certain kind of practice of prayer. Why this should be so will be clearer if we turn from considering those who affirm Marxism's substantial truth to considering those who assert its substantial falsity.

There have long been ample grounds for the rejection of this or that part of Marxism; what is interesting, however, is the way in which the rejection of Marxism normally entails the rejection of the possibility of constructing any view of the world which possesses the dimensions of Marxism. Not only are the moral attitudes of Marx, or the analysis of past history, or the predictions about the future abandoned; so is the possibility of any doctrine which connects moral attitudes, beliefs about the past, and beliefs in future possibility. The lynch pin of this rejection is the liberal belief that facts are one thing, values another—and that the two realms are logically independent of each other. This belief underpins the liberal rejection of Christianity as well as the liberal rejection of Marxism. For the liberal, the individual being the source of all value necessarily legislates for himself in matters of value; his autonomy is only preserved if he is regarded as *choosing* his own ultimate principles, unconstrained by any external consideration. But for both Marxism and Christianity only the answer to questions about the character of nature and society can provide the basis for an answer to the question: "But how ought I to live?" For the nature of the world is such that in discovering the order of things I also discover my own nature and those ends which beings such as myself must pursue if we are not to be frustrated in certain predictable ways. Knowledge of nature and society is thus the principal determinant of action. I shall turn now to consider the liberal alternative to this doctrine.

The same process of privatization is at work here as in the case of the adherents of Marxism. The triviality of Marxism held only as a set of private moral opinions is in part the outcome of the status accorded to all private moral opinions in a liberal society. What

I mean here can be brought out by considering the weakness of the position of those Marxists who have from time to time broken their ties with the Communist movement on moral grounds. Consider the moral revulsion that was felt over the Soviet intervention in Hungary or the Hitler-Stalin pact or over such episodes as the handing over to the Gestapo by the Russian government in 1940 of almost one hundred Austrian, German and Hungarian Communists. A Communist who broke with his Party on account of such an action, and who did so not merely because he felt such actions to be imprudent from the Communist standpoint, but because he believed them to be wrong, was and is peculiarly vulnerable to the questions: "What do you mean by 'wrong'?" and "How do you justify a belief that some action is wrong?" The moral framework within which members of his own society operate seems to offer him only two alternatives. He may choose to take up a utilitarian attitude and say that the actions in question increase the amount of pain and unhappiness in the world and decrease the amount of happiness. He will then be challenged by his former comrades as to whether in fact the long-term effects of these actions will not increase the amount of happiness and decrease the amount of pain and unhappiness to an extent that will outweigh the short-term suffering caused. So long as the ex-Communist remains a utilitarian his only available answer to this rejoinder is to argue as to the facts. But if this is the case, there is no moral difference between him and his ex-comrades, but only one as to the facts. (On the orthodox communist side, of course, a phenomenon I have already noticed also appears: that of attaching moral value to believing that the facts are of a certain kind.) Yet to characterize the kind of change involved in passing from being a Communist to being outside the communist movement as merely a matter of coming to hold different factual beliefs seems obviously inadequate.

Suppose, then, that instead of attacking the actions of his former comrades on utilitarian grounds the ex-Communist tries to invoke certain absolute and binding principles. That is, he asserts that certain types of action simply ought not to be done and that other types of action ought to be done, whatever the predictable consequences. Then he can be asked why he adopts these principles rather than others, and what kind of authority such principles have over us. He will discover among both Anglo-Saxon moral philosophers and their continental contemporaries the view that such principles are and must be *chosen* by the individual moral agent. Whatever authority such principles have over me they have only because I have chosen to give it to them. But if this is so, what reason can others have for being impressed or moved by any moral evaluations, unless they happen accidentally to have made the same choice of ultimate principles? And in this latter case, what they are moved by is not my judgment but their own. Thus the cost of moving away from the public utilitarian framework seems to be moral privacy and moral solipsism. Indeed, the ex-Communist is bound to ask in what way contemporary liberalism has offered any moral alternative to the morality of communism. This question becomes the more pressing if we turn from the history of the orthodox Communist parties, whether in their Stalinist, Khrushchevist, or Maoist phases, where an enormous amount of gratuitous immoral action has taken place, to the history of, for example, Trotskyism which preserved the original moral framework of communism but strenuously and at great human cost opposed the concentration camps and the other tyrannies and murders of Stalinism.

In *Their Morals and Ours* Trotsky took up this very question. He denied that every and any type of action is permissible in some circumstances for a Marxist. But he did so precisely and only because he argued that the ends of communism can only be attained by the use of some means and not of others. For this reason treachery to one's own comrades is ruled out. Thus Trotsky, too, falls back into utilitarianism and transforms his moral dissent from Stalinism into a disagreement about what in fact the proximate and remote consequences of certain types of action are. Yet Trotsky's version of the utilitarian argument raises more sharply than any other the questions which exhibit the major flaws of utilitarianism. These are twofold. On the one hand, there is the question of what is to count as beneficial or harmful, as constituting happiness or its opposite. For "happiness" as utilitarians use it is a blanket term embracing whatever is a good for men. But the goods which man pursue are in fact various, heterogeneous, and conflicting; thus, we need some criterion to enable us to select among possible goals. What good and whose good shall we seek? Bentham was able to believe that he could answer this question because he thought that he was able to provide a quantitative criterion, so that we could say how much pleasure a given activity or experience involved. But this belief that human goods can be measured against each other by means of some quantitative scale is the belief that human goods can be assessed in a way analogous to that by which commodities have a monetary value. For just this reason Marx saw Bentham as a philosopher with the mind of a small shopkeeper. No one was more conscious than Marx of the existence of rival and incompatible sets of goods; indeed this is for him a necessary counterpart to the existence of classes with conflicting interests.

The second major incoherence of utilitarianism is closely related to the first. If we have once detached ourselves from the Benthamite illusion that happiness or pleasure consists in the having of certain sensations, then it is clear that we have to distinguish between those activities which are carried out only as a means to something else and those activities which are worthwhile in themselves. A doctrine like Marxism which puts its political and moral goals in the future is not thereby delayed from seeing the possibility of living as men ought to live as realizable, if only for some men and in a partial and deformed way, in the present. It is clear that Marx saw this, and equally clear that the utilitarian attention to consequences rather than to actions themselves is liable to lead to a continuous evaluation of the present only as it leads on to some future. Marx's original criticisms of alienation and of class society rely upon a notion of unalienated man which provides a standard by which the present is judged and found wanting. But although

the final defeat of alienation may lie in the future, it
is possible to overcome the distortion of one's own
life in the present to a greater or lesser degree. It is
quite false that Marx's own judgments were directed
only to the future consequences of present actions.
Marx condemned and hated the rise of servility for
what that quality was in a man, not just for its effects;
and he admired and praised the heroic virtues of the
Paris Commune in spite of the fact that he judged its
conduct of its affairs ill-calculated so far as future
consequences were concerned. If Marx then neither
in theory nor in practice was a utilitarian, how did
utilitarianism come to dominate the Marxist movement?

It did so because of the way in which Marxism
was overcome by and assimilated itself to the modes
of thought of the very society of which it sought to be
a critique. We can distinguish two relevant stages in
this assimilation. First of all, there is the would-be dis-
carding of Marxism's Hegelian inheritance and with
it the loss of that particular view of human nature
upon which Marx's own moral critique had depended. Then there is, in consequence, the stage at
which to ask the question why a man ought to become
a revolutionary socialist, or a socialist at all, becomes
an embarrassment. This embarrassment is strikingly

exhibited in the exchange between Bernstein and Kautsky over morals. Because he saw the accomplishment of socialist goals as no longer providing adequate motivation for socialists (since he believed those goals to be probably unattainable), Bernstein fell back on an appeal to Kantian moral imperatives derived from an objective and timeless moral law. In so doing, of course, he broke with Marxism even more certainly than he had done in rejecting Marx's predictions about the downfall of capitalism. For Marx had seen belief in such a moral law as part of the false consciousness of alienated man, and he had argued that the function of such beliefs was to conceal the fact of changing and conflicting systems of values. But although Kautsky had no difficulty in criticizing Bernstein's moral views, the crudity and emptiness of his own, which turn out to be nothing other than one more version of utilitarianism, are inescapable.

I have now said enough to prepare the way for the statement of a third possibility, which I earlier suggested exists in addition to the possibilities of simply accepting or simply rejecting Marxism. My criticisms of those who accept orthodox Marxism have been both factual and moral; my criticisms of those who reject it is that what they accept in exchange for Marxism as a way of life in a secularized liberal society turns out to be that very same moral outlook which belonged there when they were Marxists. But I have also suggested that this was because, in time, Marxism took on the moral color of its surroundings and that in Marx we can perceive at least in outline the shape of a different view. But it has also been clear that this moral view cannot be detached from the view of human nature and society of which it forms a part. We shall profit most if we see this total view in the following way.

The bourgeois society of the nineteenth century articulated itself in terms of concepts and beliefs, which, although they took on differing theoretical forms, were all part of the apparatus of secular liberalism. Liberalism is the theoretical mirror in which the nineteenth century was able to see its own face; and just as the social structures of the nineteenth century depend upon division and compartmentalization, so liberal theory similarly develops a view of the world as divided and compartmentalized. The most fundamental of the distinctions inherent in liberalism is that between the political and the economic. Just as in its actual social practice the bourgeoisie's goal is that of a purely negative, non-interventionist relationship between the state—conceived narrowly as a device for protecting the citizen from foreign invasion and internal disorder and for upholding the sanctity of contract—and the economy of the free market, so in liberal political theory it is thought possible to divorce a man's political status from his economic status. Thus liberalism can combine within itself a drive towards ideals of political equality with an actual fostering of economic inequality. And just as the political is separated from the economic, so morality, too, tends to become a realm apart, a realm concerned with private relationships. There occurs the break that E. M. Forster noted between the private world of a personal culture and the public world of telegrams and anger.

Marx is in the first instance a critic of liberalism and of bourgeois society in their own terms. He approaches bourgeois society not as an external critic, but as one who tries to show first the incoherence and falsity of the account which bourgeois society gives of itself in the form of liberal theory, and secondly, how both theory and social forms contain within themselves the seeds of their own transcendence. Marx as a critic of bourgeois society can be contrasted usefully with both Carlyle and Ruskin. The evils of early capitalism, against which Marx and Engels revolted, they characterize in terms remarkably similar to those of Carlyle. But Carlyle's moralism, his invocations of duty, must have seemed to them an attempt to invoke just the kind of empty and formal category with which the ruling classes were most at home. Ruskin is much closer to Marx and Engels in his wish to close the gap between the industrial and the aesthetic. But Marx saw, as neither Carlyle nor Ruskin did, the liberating as well as the frustrating aspects of a capitalist economy and society. When Ruskin saw in the forms and effects of the division of labor characteristic of a capitalist economy only what was frustrating and distorting, Marx saw also the necessary concomitants of a development of industry of the kind that could alone provide the basis for a mass political and economic democracy.

In his economics Marx is the pupil of Ricardo and his true innovations are not so much *within* economics as in refusing to allow the categories of economics to come between us and the actual workings of social systems. It is not surprising that sociologists have been able to learn much more from Marx than have economists. We can characterize Marx's relationship to Ricardo and to Adam Smith in the following way: They, remaining within narrowly economic categories and viewing society as a total *economic* system, envisaged the different classes in society as differentiated by function, each performing its cooperative part in producing a common outcome. Marx insists upon viewing classes not in terms of their role in a theoretical schematism but as social realities, as collections of human beings whose intentions spring not only from the role assigned to them by an economic system but from their total human nature. Starting from this premise Marx sees class conflict, not class cooperation, as endemic in capitalism. Thus Marx's class analysis springs from his refusal to separate political man or economic man from social man, and his consequent ability to identify conflicts of interest which the self-description embodied in bourgeois social forms and in liberal theory observed by uses of language which made the existence of an overriding common interest appear as a necessity of thought, independent of contingent social realities.

In liberalism's reification of purely economic categories Marx saw the counterpart for bourgeois society of those reifications which, in earlier society, took a religious form. Where divine necessity appeared to rule the fate of ancient Greeks, or divine predestination that of sixteenth- and seventeenth-century Calvinists, the impersonal iron laws of the economy appeared to rule the fate of nineteenth-century employers and workers. Marx's demythologizing of this doctrine seems to have been thought by some later

Marxists to have rid us of this kind of reification once and for all; but it is my argument here that Marxism itself has too often been remythologized. Originally a negative, skeptical, and subversive doctrine in liberal society, Marxism acquired, as it became a positive doctrine, precisely that kind of attachment to its own categories which it had already diagnosed in liberal theory as one of the sources of liberalism's inability to view society except through the distorting lenses of its own categories. Furthermore, the very fact that Marxism criticizes liberalism and bourgeois society from within means that Marxism not only transcends, but also perpetuates certain liberal categories of thought.

Lukacs, in *History and Class Consciousness*, argued that historical materialism could not exempt itself from the treatment it accorded to all other doctrines. It is a central truth of historical materialism that all philosophical theories in some way or other bear the marks of the period in which they were first brought to birth. If this is true, Lukacs inquired, what traces of its period of origin are found in historical materialism itself? The most important part of his answer concerns the relationship between the economic and the political within the Marxist schematism. For Marx in some later formulations—and much more clearly for Engels and for Plekhanov—the political forms part of the superstructure of society while economic activity constitutes its basis. Since basis and superstructure stand in an external, contingent, causal relationship to each other, they must be separate, and separately identifiable realms. The Engels-Plekhanov version of historical materialism wishes to use this basis-superstructural model in the analysis of all societies, with the economic as the universally determining factor, even if, as Engels added with a note of caution in a letter to Bloch, it is so "only in the last analysis." Lukacs argues that historical materialists in following this procedure are trying to apply to all societies a form of analysis that is applicable only to classical bourgeois society. That is to say, the separation between the state and the free market economy in bourgeois practice is reflected not only in the analytical categories of liberalism, but also in those of Marxism. And perhaps this is true of Marxism to a greater extent than Lukacs believed.

Consider, for example, two other interrelated themes. One is the concept of class which Marx derived from Adam Smith and Ricardo, and which he only partially transformed. Marx's explicit and implicit definitions of class are not always the same, but he bequeathed to his heirs the notion that a class is to be defined in terms of its relationship to the ownership of the means of production. The notion of ownership itself is worth scrutiny, but never receives it in classical Marxist contexts. For since ownership is a legal notion and the law is peculiarly apt to breed social fictions, a definition of social class in terms of ownership is likely to lead precisely to that substitution of the ideal for the real which Marx condemned; so the ideal has been substituted for the real in just this way in Communist states. The alleged classlessness, or approach to classlessness, in these states consists in the fact that all citizens share in the legal "ownership" of the productive resources. But the real and very different relationships of different sections of the population to the political, social, and economic control of these resources and to the decision-making process involved are only masked by this appeal to the fiction of "ownership" with its roots in the interests of the actually ruling group. If Marxism in this respect, too, betrays the defects of its nineteenth-century origins, it is partly at a loss because, just as it was Marx's subtlety and flexibility over class that was lost in the notion his successors took over, so also crudity conquered subtlety in relation to questions of ideology.

For Marx the ideology of a given society is that image of itself which its social forms necessarily engender; it is a society's self-consciousness, at once revealing and distorting. But Marxism was intended to be an anti-ideology, a critical instrument for unmasking such distortions. However, because Marxists have been unable to be sufficiently self-critical of their own conceptual schemes, Marxism became available as a conservative ideology the moment social forms appeared which were undeniably different from those of classical capitalism and which were prepared to utilize a Marxist vocabulary for the purposes of self-description. At this point the emptiness of the characterization of socialism and communism by Marx, which we have already noticed as springing from Marx's unwillingness to prescribe for others in advance, made it all the easier for the state capitalist bureaucracy of the U.S.S.R. to wear a Marxist mask. Honest Marxists of the Trotskyist tradition saw clearly that this involved the subversive redefinition of some basic Marxist concepts. But on the positive characterization of bureaucracy specifically, Marxist analyses have been notably weak. This has not only affected Marxist analysis of the Soviet bloc; it has also weakened understanding of the bureaucratic neo-capitalism of the West.

If I have been preoccupied up to this point with the weaknesses of Marxism, it is partly because of the urgency of the task of providing for contemporary society a critique on the scale of Marx's critique of classical capitalism. I have in effect argued in this book that Marx's inheritance from Christianity was twofold. On the one hand, he brought down to earth the hitherto metaphysical themes of alienation, and used them for concrete and illuminating analyses; on the other hand, by insisting on the possibility of a more than empiricist understanding of social facts, he laid himself open to the possibility of the very reification, the very false consciousness in his own theorizing that he had seen to be inseparable from religious modes of thought. The only way of showing that it is possible to rescue Marxism from its errors, and still to retain those truths about the human condition which cannot as yet be found elsewhere, would be to actively carry through the type of contemporary critique I have proposed.

The need for such a critique is clear from at least three distinct points of view. The first is that of Marxism itself, which in the absence of such a critique continually breeds degenerated forms of itself. Some of these are the doctrines of those who, because of the gap between the classical Marxist analysis and the realities of contemporary society, flee from the realities of that society into the private cloud-cuckoo lands of

Marxist sectarianism where they tilt at capitalist wind-mills with Marxist texts in their hands, the Don Quixotes of the contemporary left. Other degen-erated forms of Marxism are the doctrines of those who, because of that very same gap, embrace what Lenin called the worship of what is. They give a new sense to key terms in Marxist theory, equating Marx's notion of authentically free labor with that of the shortening of the working day, as some Soviet Marx-ists do, or, like Isaac Deutscher, allowing Marx's no-tion of revolutionary working-class power to be confused with that of the administrative maneuvers of the Soviet bureaucrats.

The second point of view from which such a critique is necessary is that of contemporary social science. Talcott Parsons has pointed out the extensive influence of Marxism on American sociology, but this influence has been notably unsystematic. Yet in the Hegelian and Marxist tradition we find, as I have ar-gued earlier, a schematism for analyzing societies in terms of their potentialities for realizing certain goals accepted by certain groups, only at the cost of dis-solving the established social order. The resources for genuine theory construction embodied in the Marxist tradition are as yet largely unused and undis-cussed by social scientists. But it is not only for the sake of the internal development of social science that this failure is to be regretted. The whole Marxist attempt to envisage societies from the standpoint of their openness to the future, of the possibilities of development inherent in them, runs counter to the spirit of an age in which the future is always conceived of as a larger edition of the present. It is important to be able to combat that spirit, if the virtue of hope is to survive in a secular form.

Finally, to return to a central theme: such a critique is important for contemporary Christianity. Nothing has been more startling than to note how much contemporary Christian theology is concerned with trying to perform Feuerbach's work all over again. For if Christianity, in even the semi-secular society of the present, is to be able to present itself as having a relevant content and function, it is forced to present itself as having a secular content and function. Hence the many attempts to demythologize Christianity, to separate relevant kernel from irrelevant husk. The tragedy of these attempts is that what is disentangled as the essential human meaning of Christianity is so platitudinous, and it is platitudinous precisely because what is presented is a way of life in accordance with the liberal values and illiberal realities of the established order. That function of religion which consisted in providing a radical criticism of the secular present is lost by those contemporary demythologizers whose goal is to assimilate Christianity to the secular present. But this is not a necessary outcome of the attempt to realize the human meaning of the Christian gospels. It is a basic contention of this book that Hegel, Feuerbach, and Marx humanized certain central Christian beliefs in such a way as to present a secularized version of the Christian judgment upon, rather than the Christian adaptation to, the secular present. It is sad that the demythologizers of the gospel are often anxious to free Christianity from its inheritance from Gnosticism, but worry far less about what Christianity inherited from Pontius Pilate and Caiaphas. If they are to learn to do otherwise, it is difficult to believe that they will not have to learn from both the achievements and the failures of Marxism.